The Real Deal

Property Invest Your Way to Financial Freedom!

BRENDAN KELLY & SIMON BUCKINGHAM

Macquarie
Regional Library

Wrightbooks

First published 2010 by Wrightbooks
an imprint of John Wiley & Sons Australia, Ltd
42 McDougall Street, Milton Qld 4064
Office also in Melbourne

Typeset in Berkeley Oldstyle Book 11.3/14pt

© Brendan Kelly and Simon Buckingham 2010

The moral rights of the authors have been asserted

National Library of Australia Cataloguing-in-Publication data:

Author:	Kelly, Brendan
Title:	The real deal: property invest your way to financial freedom/ Brendan Kelly and Simon Buckingham.
ISBN:	9781742469836 (pbk.)
Notes:	Includes index.
Subjects:	Real estate investment — Australia.
	Real estate investment — New Zealand.
	Real estate business — Australia.
	Real estate business — New Zealand.
	Finance, Personal — Australia.
	Finance, Personal — New Zealand.
	House buying — Australia.
	House buying — New Zealand
Other Authors/ Contributors:	Buckingham, Simon.
Dewey Number:	332.63240994

Cover images © Vision; © Photodisc; © PhotoEssentials; © Kutlaev Dmitry, 2010. Used under licence from Shutterstock.com.

Printed in China by Printplus Limited

10 9 8 7 6 5 4 3 2 1

Disclaimer

Contents

Part II: Renovations

Part III: Subdivisions plus

Part IV: Construction

Part V: Systemisation

Foreword

The most powerful confirmation that an investing concept works is the personal testimony of someone who has applied the technique and succeeded in creating a profitable outcome.

This is why I'm delighted to recommend *The Real Deal* as a refreshingly good read that combines sensible and interesting investing principles with illustrations of real-life investors who have been able to apply the points made and make decent profits.

The people featured in this book are everyday people, and most started with little or no investing background or experience. Take 23-year-old Rachel (chapter 3), for example. Rachel is probably more at home on a surfboard than inspecting properties, but her lack of starting knowledge was more than overcome by a strong desire to learn, an inquisitive mind, and the tenacity to keep asking questions until she received an answer that made sense. Now she owns a great property investment and has established a solid foundation for a strong financial future.

The 14 success stories included in *The Real Deal* were drawn from RESULTS participants. RESULTS is a mentoring program that teams those wanting to use real estate to achieve financial freedom with an experienced property investing mentor, while providing substantial written training materials and other forms of support.

Although I was involved in its creation, through the excellent work of Simon Buckingham, Brendan Kelly and others, RESULTS has been significantly refined and improved. As you read the impressive accounts of how profits were made in the upcoming pages, remember that the circumstances of each contributor are different, but participating in RESULTS and leveraging off the knowledge and support of their RESULTS mentor is something that unites them all.

As you progress through this book I urge you to look for applications for how you can achieve similar results to those featured. Don't dwell on how you're different as a reason for why property investing won't or can't work for you. Instead, see the person behind the story—their desire to do something different; how they overcame adversity; who helped them along the way; and what success has meant to them.

It's impossible not to be inspired by *The Real Deal*, and I'm certain that by the time you've finished you will have gained many new and profitable investing insights and a double dose of motivation to pursue the financial freedom you know you deserve.

God bless,

Steve McKnight
#1 best-selling author of *From 0 to 130 Properties in 3.5 Years.*

About the authors

Simon Buckingham

I was once in the 9 am to 5 pm (or more like the 7 am to 7 pm!) rat race, dreaming of something more, as you might be. I was working extremely hard, and I hated it.

Every Sunday from about 2 o'clock in the afternoon I'd start to get a sinking feeling in the pit of my stomach, thinking about the heavy workload and ungrateful clients that I would have to face in the week ahead. It was soul-destroying. I wasn't happy, and I knew my future held more of the same for many years if I didn't take action.

I was painfully aware of how much time I was spending doing things I didn't enjoy. I desperately wanted my time back and to have more control over what I did each day. I wanted to escape the rat race.

Picking up a Robert Kiyosaki book while Christmas shopping one year was a turning point. I read the back cover, and thought, 'Hey, this book is all about me!' I read it in one weekend, and came to the realisation that if I could earn more through investing than I spend I would be financially free. I suddenly felt like the doors had opened on a whole new world, and I started to see all sorts of opportunities around me. I began to look into real estate investing and attended several seminars. At a Steve McKnight seminar everything started to come together and make sense, and the very next day I bought my first investment property. Since then I've never looked back.

Many properties later I was approached by Steve McKnight and his business partner Dave Bradley about a mentoring program they were putting together. Seeing the opportunity to expand my skills and also pass on what I had learnt to help other people create better lives for themselves, I jumped in with both feet.

I now invest regularly in property and business, and also run property programs and coach other investors. In the past six years I have done over 45 property deals using multiple strategies, including positive cash flow, subdivisions, developments and commercial property. These days my investing is all about giving me more time to spend with my family and on the things that I love doing.

Brendan Kelly

If you were to speak to my parents, I think they'd tell you that I've been searching for 'my purpose' for most of my life. Over the years they've watched me evolve with a certain amount of trial and error. For example, I've been a taxi driver, model, maths teacher, insurance agent, salesperson, warehousing and distribution manager, carpenter ... They've seen me work on the tools, in a classroom, on a production line, on the shop floor and in an office. However, there's something that they knew long before I did: teaching has always been in my heart!

After many years in universities, while still searching for 'my purpose', I began the slow and somewhat thankless climb up the corporate ladder—until my first child was born. This amazing event had a significant impact on my life: it was the trigger for me to take a hard look at the path my life was taking.

I realised that superannuation was not the answer as it wouldn't provide enough money for a comfortable retirement. I realised that opportunities as an employee would be limited to the willingness of my boss to promote me. If I was to provide all that I wanted for myself and my family, and be happy along the way, some significant changes would need to occur.

With the blessing of my wife, I left a senior management role overseeing 24 staff and a $20 million inventory and said goodbye to a six-figure salary. I finished up work on the Friday and had a hammer and nails in my hands on Monday morning, working on my first dedicated renovation for profit.

It's funny how things begin to fall into place when you make a commitment and take action! Shortly after I began on this new path, I was approached by Steve McKnight and David Bradley and was engaged as the first ever Property Coach for the RESULTS Mentoring Program.

This was it! The search was over!

For me, it's all about property coaching and hands-on investing.

Now, like Simon, I regularly invest in property and business, run property programs and coach other investors. In fact, I've now coached over 600 people in real estate investing, from all walks of life! (It turns out that all that trial and error had a purpose—I can appreciate almost anyone's current circumstances.)

Because I took on the challenge of making a change in direction, I am now on a path that makes a difference, fills my life, and provides all that I want for myself and my family.

Acknowledgements

There are a large number of people who have contributed either directly or indirectly to the creation of this book. Each deserves recognition for the role that they have played in our lives, in our investing and business activities, in the mentoring program we run, and specifically for their help in putting together the pages you are about to read.

This book represents a culmination of knowledge and experience from the authors and the contributors, who have generously donated their stories, their time and their wisdom to make this book about real people doing real deals. In chapter order, we'd like to recognise Matt and Amanda, Jane, Rachel, Matt and Tiere, Gladys, Troy S, Katie, Shilpa, David, Colleen, Mandy, Adam, Trevor, and Troy H, for your sincerity and integrity. You have been extraordinary supporters of this book and the RESULTS Mentoring community at large. Thank you.

In addition, and without reservation, the assistance we have received from Michael has been nothing short of extraordinary. Your patience and guidance has helped make this book a reality. Thank you, Michael!

Special thanks need to go to Candace. Your dogged support for both of us in managing our lives around the creation of this book has not gone unnoticed! Also to the team in the office: Leon, Goldie, Emy, Renee, Lisa, Normie, Naomi ... thanks for all your generous support and encouragement over the years!

We'd like to offer our sincerest appreciation and gratitude to Steve McKnight and Jeremy Thomas who continue to contribute to our success and drive to achieve. Without them, this book would still be just a dream.

Thanks must also be given to Katherine and the team at John Wiley & Sons. You have consistently encouraged and supported everything we have wanted this book to be.

To our families, thank you for your support and (at times extreme) patience over the months of writing this book. Julie and Lynn, you are our loves, lives and worlds! Thank you for being such fantastic mothers to our children James, Aaron, Aidan and Amelie. Our parents, too, should be acknowledged for their unconditional love and for instilling in us the belief that we can be anything we want to be.

All royalties for this book are donated to Whitelion, a charity that works closely with disadvantaged young people to give them greater opportunities in life. Special thanks must go to Mark Watt, Whitelion's CEO, whose dedication and passion in supporting youth at risk is truly inspiring.

And far from least ... thank *you*.

You have chosen to invest in your own education and to take yet another step towards living the life that you most desire. We believe that this is what it's all about ... learning, persistence and taking action! Well done for making the commitment to yourself to keep going.

May you achieve success beyond your wildest dreams!

Preface

Do you wake up each morning and dread going to work?

Do you lie awake at night thinking there must be a way to create a better life for yourself?

Do you have big goals but don't know how to reach them?

You might have a dream of financial freedom but have no idea how to achieve it. By now you might have figured out that working 9 to 5 won't get you there; being self-employed may not either. Investing in the sharemarket might work but you have no say in how that business is run. There is a way for you to take control of your own destiny and achieve everything you ever dreamed of: investing in real estate.

Property gives you possibilities that no other form of investment does. There are deals that will make a quick profit, deals that will earn you passive income, deals that you can work on yourself and deals that you can pay others to look after for you. Short-term deals. Long-term deals. Big. Small. You can combine strategies and come up with your own truly unique deals. The options are really only limited by your own creativity. This is what makes property a great way to reach financial freedom: whatever your personal goals and circumstances, there's an approach that will work for you.

In *The Real Deal* we're going to introduce you to a number of different real estate investing strategies, and then in each chapter we're going to hear from a real investor who has used that approach to create wealth for themselves. These are people who are just like you. They once got up every morning and trudged off to work, so that they could put food on the table, petrol in the car and clothes on the kids. And they also dreamed of something more. They have that same itch that you have, the idea that there must be a way to get more out of life than this!

There is. The people in this book have found it, and you can too.

As you read through the deals, be encouraged by the fact that these are normal people. They didn't start out as property gurus, have millions of dollars to invest or mountains of free time on their hands to get started. Before starting out in property most of them were working in average jobs with average incomes, and knew little or nothing about real estate. Many of them were nervous about making their first investments, and experienced some anxiety along the way. But they could also see that they were taking their first steps towards their goals, and they weren't going to turn back. And just to show you that these people aren't super-powered real estate juggernauts, you will also read about a few deals that went south. Just like a successful deal, a failed deal provides valuable lessons. These investors have learned a lot from their errors, and you will too.

Finding your *why*

Ultimately you are not investing for the fun of it (although many people do find it fun), you are investing because you want to improve your quality of life by reducing or eliminating the need to work.

What does financial freedom mean to you?

Do you want to sit on the beach all day reading Patricia Cornwell novels? Do you want to travel the world? Or simply spend more time with your family? We call this finding your *why*.

If your answer is simply 'to make more money', you have little chance of success. Everyone encounters obstacles on their investing journey, and the goal of simply 'making money' will not be enough to help navigate these problems.

When trouble hits you can think about how good it will feel to sit on the beach while everybody else is at work, spend more time with your family, pick up the keys to your Porsche or drive to the airport to catch your flight to France. This will get you going again. This will keep you motivated. This will keep you inspired.

Real estate investing can provide freedom, security and a good lifestyle. It's a journey for life, not a get-rich-quick process. Why are *you* taking the journey?

Introduction

People come to property investing from all sorts of backgrounds and with differing levels of skill and experience, but they often have the same goal: financial freedom.

In *The Real Deal* you are going to read about different real estate investing methods. Each chapter examines a different strategy, and each real deal shows how this works in real life. Each person and each story is different, and together they provide valuable insights into how to make a property deal successful.

The strategies grow more complicated as the book progresses. This is deliberate. It follows the path of a typical investor, starting out with a straightforward rental property or renovation, progressing through subdivision and often advancing to developments and commercial properties.

This is a journey of increasing complexity and—if done correctly—increasing profit.

You'll also notice that the book is broken up into parts. The design here is to help you categorise the different investing strategies and make your decision-making process easier so that you can pick the right strategy for you.

On the road to financial freedom...

Nothing good in life comes without effort.

What is financial freedom?

Financial freedom is achieved when the income from your investments exceeds your living costs, so that you no longer have to work. It's that simple! It means not having to worry about money; you can make decisions based on what you *want* to do, rather than what you can *afford* to do. You will still have to put some time and effort into managing your investments, but we think you'll agree that spending a day a week on your properties is much better than spending five days a week at work.

Financial freedom is not the same as being rich. It's all about earning more from investments than you spend. If your aim in life is simply to be able to surf all day, you could be financially free earning $50000 per year from your investments. If your goal is to travel extensively, perhaps you need $120000 each year because this lifestyle will cost more. Everybody's financial needs are different. If you don't need to spend much, you don't need to earn much.

On the road to financial freedom...

When your income from your investments exceeds your expenses you can quit your job!

The property investing journey

If you are planning on taking the property investing journey, chances are you're not enjoying what you do now. Maybe you've had enough of working 7 am to 7 pm for a boss who doesn't remember your name half the time, in a job that dominates your life. Think about what it is you want most: to spend more time with your family, to buy a Ferrari or a new Ducati motorbike, or to drive around Europe in a sports car. Is it your dream to see New York but you just can't afford it? Or maybe you just want to make sure that you can live a good life in retirement.

Now think about your current situation. Do you feel stuck in a rut? Do you lie awake at night thinking there must be more to life? Do you have the all-too-common Sunday arvo dreads, where on Sunday afternoon work starts to weigh on your mind as you think about the week ahead, and you wish you could just hide under the bed? These are all signs of discomfort. But, far from being a problem, these are *good* signs: they mean that you are ready to change. They mean that you are ready to chase your *why*.

On the road to financial freedom...

If you are feeling discomfort, that's a good thing. It means you are ready to make a change.

So, how do you do this?

The first step in your property investing journey is taking action to combat this discomfort. You can attend a property investing seminar, talk to a real estate agent, do some research on the internet, read a property investment book (hey ... well done!). Even if it's just a tiny step, you must take positive action that will be the beginning of your property investing journey. You must show yourself and the world that you are serious.

Your discomfort is telling you that what you are doing is not working, so do something about it!

Once you have begun to make things happen, you must keep them happening. Reaching your dreams will require effort and commitment; everything worthwhile in life does. Think about your *why*, and how exciting it will be to achieve it. Use these thoughts and feelings whenever you hit a rough patch. If a deal falls through, or you don't get a property you thought would be perfect for you, or a tenant sets fire to one of your units with a home-made fireplace, use this feeling to keep things on track. Such problems are certain to occur; if your desire is stronger than the obstacles you face, you will come out on top. If not, you are much more likely to stumble on the road to financial freedom.

After you've started to make changes in your life, you must stay the course and withstand any resistance you might feel from those around you. Maybe you have been spending your nights and weekends researching deals and educating yourself about property. Maybe you've already made your first deal. Whatever steps you have started to take towards your goal of financial freedom, those around you who have similar desires but are not taking action may begin to show some resistance to your success. They'll question what you are doing. This often takes the form of comments such as, 'You can't leave your job, it provides steady income', 'Who do you think you are, Bill Gates?', 'You don't have enough money to do that', or 'You're doing something really good, and I wish I was doing it too, but I'm not, so I'm going to be difficult and sulk and criticise what you are doing so that maybe you'll stop and then I won't have to feel bad about not doing anything'. Okay, so you probably won't hear that last one, but really this is exactly what such comments mean. Can you handle this?

On the road to financial freedom...

The more resistance you face, the more committed you must be. This also means you are doing something right. Little resistance can mean your dreams may not be big enough.

You will most likely still be working full time in your job and spending a lot of your spare time chasing and making deals or educating yourself, or staying at home eating baked beans by candlelight to save money. Are you willing to make such short-term sacrifices for long-term gain? If you are, then you will start to see rewards for your effort. Maybe your first deal will be completed and you will bank a tidy profit, or you find a tenant for the property you have renovated and the rent cheques start coming in. How exciting!

It can then be tempting to get comfortable again. But if you're committed, very soon you'll start to feel that what you've done so far, while a great start, won't get you to where you want to be, and it's time to take another step forwards. This repeated discomfort is an essential part of the process. It is what spurs you to keep going, and is likely to happen many times before you reach your *why*.

On the road to financial freedom...

'The enemy of a great life is a good life.'
Brendan Nichols

On the flipside, if it takes you six months to get your life and finances in order, that's six months very well spent. The wiser path is not to start out until you are ready, financially and emotionally, for the road ahead.

Bill Gates and Richard Branson both created their fortunes from nothing. They weren't born into wealth. They didn't inherit the family business. But they do both have an overwhelming passion for wealth. You have the same potential to achieve as these two. Bill Gates and Richard Branson only have 24 hours in a day, and they both clean their teeth, eat breakfast and sleep—just like you. You must believe that you deserve it or you will never achieve it. The achievement of your first deal will inspire you, and your confidence will increase exponentially. This will help you to keep going. Persistence is the key.

On the road to financial freedom...

Property is just an investing vehicle. What is more important is the destination that your vehicle is going to get you to.

Choosing the right strategy for you

It's up to you to decide what strategy is best for you, but you are not on your own. For your convenience, at the beginning of each chapter we've put together a summary of how the following issues relate to each strategy. This is designed to give you valuable information to help you assess different approaches to investing in property. We think it's important to take into account:

➤ your goals

➤ your skill level and experience

➤ the amount of time you can devote to your investing

➤ the amount of cash you have available

➤ your borrowing capacity and income.

You'll see at the start of each chapter we've used low, medium and high to describe the level of skill and experience, cash, borrowing capacity and time required for the strategy outlined in that chapter.

Also, within the chapter you will read about how the investors in this book chose the approach that suited them.

On the road to financial freedom...

It's not about getting rich quick, it's about solving the puzzle of wealth creation to create a better life for yourself.

In order to better support your understanding, let's simplify the approaches of different property investing strategies.

Hands on versus hands off

There are two different approaches to doing real estate deals: hands on and hands off.

Hands-on deals require more of your involvement, whether it is doing the work for a renovation or subdivision, negotiating a subdivision deal with the council, or project managing a development. Hands-off deals require less involvement.

With a hands-on deal you can often control how hands on the deal actually is. For example, you can employ somebody else to manage the deal for you: if you are undertaking a structural construction project you could hire a builder, or if you are undertaking a renovation you could hire a decorator. This will reduce the amount of time you have to spend on the deal. This does not mean you can forget about the project though. Keeping a close eye on your investment is crucial for it to succeed: even if they are good at what they do, people you hire will not have the same desire for the project to succeed as you do and will therefore not be as diligent as you would.

Hands-off deals require minimal time and energy from the investor. Buy and hold is the most common form of hands-off deal. You do of course have to put in the effort to find a good deal, but once this has been done a buy and hold deal is almost 'set and forget'. You are profiting from the rent paid by the tenants and (hopefully) the growth in value of the property, neither of which require regular input from you. You can also reduce your involvement in any type of deal by delegating certain tasks and responsibilities, although you should always maintain control. Ultimately the responsibility for the success of any deal lies with you.

On the road to financial freedom...

If you are not prepared to put in the time to find and manage profitable deals, perhaps property is not for you.

Another factor to consider when choosing a strategy is the outcome you are after. Is it a cash lump-sum (or capital gain) or regular cash flow that you seek from your next deal?

Lump-sum gain versus cash flow

One approach to achieve your goal and live your *why* could be to do lump-sum deals first to build up your investing funds. Once your pool of investing money is big enough, you can buy properties that produce cash flow in order to receive regular income that can replace your salary from your job.

In order to support you in your investing, at the start of every chapter we'll identify whether each deal is hands on or hands off and cash flow or lump-sum. This is designed to help you identify whether or not you might like to try this strategy.

Let's have a look at some examples:

➤ Renovations: hands on for cash lump-sum.

➤ Developments: hands on for cash lump-sum.

➤ Negatively geared buy and hold: hands off for cash lump-sum (by way of a capital gain upon selling).

➤ Positively geared buy and hold: hands off for cash flow.

Cost versus complexity and risk

To help you further with your strategy selection, at the beginning of each chapter we have included a graph comparing the cost with the risk/complexity of each deal. Here is an example:

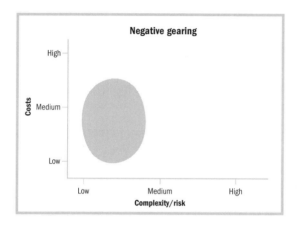

This graph for negative gearing shows that the complexity and risk for this strategy is low, and that the costs can range from low to high, depending on the deal. For example, a negatively geared unit on the outskirts of town will have a low cost to buy into, and a low cost for holding it. The process of buying a unit isn't hard, and it requires little ongoing effort. Contrast this against a house in Bondi. Such a purchase will cost a lot more to buy into and a lot more to hold. But even in this case the process is simple. It requires little ongoing effort and will likely produce the result you are after just by holding onto it.

Therefore negative gearing sits in a price range from low to high, but remains a low-risk deal irrespective of the value of the property.

This tool is also designed to help you select what approach might be right for you. But the decision is yours. Take a moment now, and in the graph below draw a circle for where you feel comfortable with the amount of cash you have available to invest in your deal and how much risk you are willing to take on. For example, on this blank graph if you have only a small amount of cash or equity (say around $40 000 to $70 000) and you are nervous about the market then you might want to circle the area that represents low costs and low complexity/risk. If you feel you have more cash or equity (hundreds of thousands of dollars) and are looking to aggressively invest, you might be happier circling a spot on the graph where high costs meets high complexity/risk. The trick then is to marry your graph here with the appropriate matching graph at the start of one of the chapters.

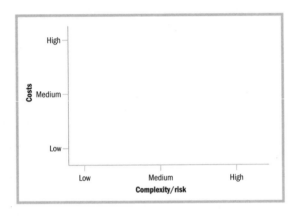

You must decide whether you are looking to take on low or high complexity/risk deals, and whether you have a small or large amount of cash to put towards a deal. Once you have made these decisions, the graphs at the beginning of each chapter can help you assess each strategy and whether it is suitable for you.

It's a good idea to have a think about what level of risk you are comfortable taking on. Do you want to go out into the deep water and chase the bigger fish? Or do you prefer to paddle in the shallows, where the catches are smaller but the risks are lower? There is no right or wrong answer, and you can be successful with both approaches if you have made a considered decision about the level of risk you are comfortable taking on, along with the skill, time and cash/equity you have at your disposal.

On the road to financial freedom...

Take the sleep test: if you constantly lie awake at night worrying about your investments, perhaps you have taken on more risk than you can handle and you might need to re-think your approach.

Part I

Buy and hold, short-term growth and flips

Chapter 1

Negative gearing for long-term growth (buy and hold)

A rental investment, or buy and hold property, might have been the first strategy you thought of when you considered getting into property investing. Just buy a property and wait for it to go up in value! And during this time the tenant pays you rent every month. Sounds great! Buy and hold doesn't require a lot of knowledge; all you need to do is be able to talk to a real estate agent and sign your name.

Most everyday property investors follow this approach, hoping the value of their investment property will appreciate (go up) over time. It is a hands-off strategy that requires little effort. What's the most common way to purchase a buy and hold investment property? Using negative gearing, which we will explain shortly.

Hands off, lump-sum cash/equity

Cash/equity requirements

- Low/medium amount of money required for a deposit and settlement costs, depending on purchase price
- Low/medium amount of money required each month to service the shortfall between rent and loan repayments

Borrowing capacity requirements

- Medium debt level dependent on price of property
- Low/medium debt servicing requirements, with rent partially offsetting interest costs

Complexity/risk

- Low complexity, low/medium risk

Skills requirements

- Low/medium levels of researching, analysis and negotiation skills will be required

Time requirements

- Medium time needed to find, negotiate and buy property
- Low time requirement after purchase
- Long time frame for making a profit

Desired outcome

- Long-term capital gain with eventual income when the debt has been substantially paid down (so that repayments are lower than the rent)

Negative gearing

Costs: High / Medium / Low

Complexity/risk: Low / Medium / High

Note: when referring to low/medium/high in these points, this is in comparison to other strategies in the book. Please refer to the introduction for an explanation of these points and the graph.

But before you even begin to think about choosing a strategy, it's time to take stock of your own circumstances. So that's where we are going to start ...

Getting started

Two of the key elements to consider when you are at the very beginning of your property investing journey are:

➤ where you want to get to

➤ where you are now.

Without goals it is difficult to have direction on your journey and you can wander around like a lost puppy: aimless, bumping into things, biting off more than you can chew and occasionally falling over. And if you haven't taken stock of your current situation, you will be lost before you even begin.

So let's have a look at addressing these two issues. We'll start with setting goals, because thinking about where you want to be will inspire you to take action.

Setting goals

An essential part of any successful investment plan is setting goals. In the preface we looked at establishing your *why*, as this will give you your ultimate goal: spending your days on the beach, buying a Ferrari or telling your boss what you really think of him as you sail off into the sunset on your new yacht, never to be seen again. (It might be a good idea to go back and read this now if you're not a person who usually reads the preface!)

Shorter term goals

Once you have established your *why*, you must work out how you are going to get there. A great way to do this is to set some shorter term goals. Rather than focusing on a target that is a long way in the future and can seem difficult to reach, you can take smaller, planned steps along the road that you know will lead to your *why*.

You can create these shorter term goals by asking the question, 'What do I need to have achieved in ...?' For example, working backwards from 12 months it would go something like this:

➤ What do I need to have achieved in 12 months to ensure I will reach my *why*?

➤ What do I need to have achieved in six months to ensure that I will achieve my 12-month goals?

➤ What do I need to have achieved in 90 days to ensure that I will achieve my six-month goals?

And so on for 30 days and then seven days.

This is living to a plan and planning with the end in mind, and is a critical difference in perspective between Joe Average and Richie Rich. It's very difficult to map out a path to your ultimate destination if you start by focusing on next week, but working backwards from the longer term goals first will clarify what needs to be done in each time frame and allow you to build incrementally towards your target once you get underway. And if you can see yourself achieving the small goals you will have more faith that the big goal is achievable as well.

SMARTIE goals

You may have heard of the SMART method of goal setting. Well, we're even smarter than that—we use a SMARTIE goal-setting process! Let's have a look:

➤ **S**pecific. The goal must be clear and well defined.

➤ **M**easurable. The goal must be quantifiable, so that you can answer the question, 'Did I reach this goal?'

For example, 'To learn about property' is not a quantifiable goal; 'To study property for three months and select a strategy' is quantifiable.

> **A***chievable.* You must be able to reach the goal if you put in the effort.

> **R***ealistic.* The goal must take into account your circumstances and resources.

> **T***ime-bound.* You must have a fixed deadline.

> **I***ntegral to self.* The goal must fit with your values and beliefs.

> **E***motional.* You must have an emotional attachment to the goal, otherwise you won't have the motivation to pursue it.

So why are these SMARTIE goals smarter?

SMART goals are intellectual goals that don't fully take account of your passions and desires. But SMARTIE goals take into consideration your values and beliefs and the passion that you have to achieve them. Goals that you are emotionally attached to will help you keep going. They will crystallise your thinking and spur you on. This belief in your goals is vital to your success, especially if times get tough.

Write your SMARTIE goals down and review them regularly. If you're on target, great! Keep going. If not, have an honest look at why you might be falling short and change what needs to be changed. If you are not reaching your short-term goals you probably won't reach your *why*, so address any problems immediately.

Reward yourself along the way for reaching significant milestones, such as a six-month goal. Nothing extravagant; you should be trying to save money! Go out for dinner and a movie with your partner, or spend a day at the beach. No, just completing your daily to-do list *doesn't* warrant a bottle of champagne!

On the road to financial freedom ...

Written goals + Accountability + Action = Success!

Write your goals down and refer to them regularly.

Hold yourself accountable for meeting them.

Take action on your goals every day, even if it's only something small.

Where are you now?

Setting your goals will help to show you where you are heading —but how can you get there if you don't know where you are now? Knowing your destination, and even having a map, are useless if you don't know where you are starting from.

Get a grip on where you are financially. This includes knowing your cash/equity position and your borrowing capacity. To work these out you must know about your income, loans, credit card debts and limits, living expenses, savings and expected expenses in the future. It's like using a compass; it can point you in the direction of where you want to go, but you can't plot your course if you don't know your current coordinates.

Assessing your financial position

You need two things for almost every property deal: cash and borrowing capacity.

When borrowing money, lenders won't finance all of a property purchase unless you can put up other properties or assets as additional security. Assuming you can demonstrate your ability to meet the repayment obligations, most lenders will be comfortable lending up to 80 per cent of the purchase price or assessed value of the property (whichever is lower). You might be able to push this to 90 per cent or maybe even

95 per cent depending upon the lender, your personal circumstances, and your willingness to pay extra for a thing called
lenders mortgage insurance.

Whatever percentage of the purchase price you can borrow,
you'll somehow have to cover the shortfall between the loan and
the price of the property. You might need to have 5 per cent,
10 per cent, 20 per cent or more of the price of the property
in cash, plus some extra dollars to cover stamp duty and other
costs (this will be discussed in detail in chapter 6).

If you have built up some equity in your home, you may be
able to draw down on the equity to help you buy an investment
property. The banks will be very happy to help (in fact, they
will be racing to your door). Using the equity in your home
can become complex and risky though, so it's very important to
assess any property investment carefully and think about what
it might mean for your own home if the deal goes badly.

How much cash can you get your hands on without selling
anything? Unfortunately for many people the answer is 'not
much'. Most people only have a very limited capacity for saving.
They tend to live to (or beyond) their income. For example, if
someone has very little cash left over while earning $50 000 a
year, they are equally likely to have very little cash left over if
they move to a new job and earn $70 000 per year. Generally
their lifestyle will change to accommodate this extra income.

If you don't have the required equity or cash, your first step
shouldn't be to rush out and buy a property but to instead start
saving. It's not very exciting, but it must be done. Have a look at
your lifestyle to see what you can cut out. For four weeks, write
down *everything* you spend money on, and the amounts. This
is all about keeping a 'money diary'. After four weeks, sit down
and go through your money diary and see what you can do
without. You'll probably be surprised at how much money you
spend on some things; for example, takeaway dinners or DVD
hire. Trim this back as much as you can. Short-term sacrifices
will bring long-term gains. If you need added motivation, think

about your *why* and how good it will be to reach it. Remember that everything that you spend money on represents time that you have to spend in your job earning that money. Now, do you *really* need to have takeaway three nights a week?

Create a budget for your family. Work out exactly how much money you have coming in and going out, and allocate money to be spent on certain items. The information you have gathered about your spending habits will help with this.

The budget you develop today will ensure that you live within your capacity to spend for as long as you stick to it. And the sense of freedom you get from knowing that the dollars are there when you need them is so very rewarding!

On the road to financial freedom ...

Search the internet for 'money-saving tips', and go to the library and find books on budgeting and managing your money. You will find plenty of them. As your grandma probably told you, a dollar saved is a dollar earned.

Assessing your borrowing capacity

There are all sorts of tools and calculators on the internet that will help you assess your borrowing capacity, and you can always talk to your bank. But here's an approach that can help you work out what you could borrow now and also what you might be able to change in order to increase your borrowing capacity before you actually need a loan.

You are probably familiar with mortgage brokers; they will meet with you and assess your financial situation, and then recommend the best lender and mortgage for you. It usually costs you nothing because the broker is paid a commission by the lender that you choose.

To get a good idea of how to maximise your borrowing capacity, make an appointment with a broker. Simply search the internet and make an appointment with one of the reputable companies. At the appointment, place all of your cards on the table. Tell the broker *everything*, and ask them to make an assessment of your borrowing capacity. Then ask them to break down how they came to this figure and what limitations you have, and take lots of notes. You now have an expert's opinion on what works for you and what works against you with respect to your borrowing capacity. This is invaluable information. Your aim is to borrow as much as possible, and so you need to present your best case when it comes to actually making an application with your bank. Going to a mortgage broker first will also alert you to any changes you need to make to your circumstances to improve your chances of receiving a loan.

Here is the most crucial point of this process: *do not ask this mortgage broker to make a loan application for you.* This is all about gathering information. All applications go on your credit record, and it is best to avoid any unnecessary applications being recorded as a large number of applications on your credit file can raise an alarm for lenders. Save the actual application for later.

On the road to financial freedom...

For lenders, loans are an exercise in risk assessment. You must convince them that their money is safe in your hands, and that it will be returned to them.

You now have some of the fundamentals to begin working out what sort of investment strategy might best suit you, but keep reading—there's more to come!

Negative gearing for long-term growth

What is negative gearing?

Let's take a look at what gearing is all about and some of the pros and cons of this strategy.

Chances are that when you buy a property, you'll need to borrow the majority of the purchase price from a bank or other lender. But money isn't free, and the lender will expect you to pay interest on the debt.

If the total of the mortgage repayments, plus the costs of managing and maintaining the property, is more than the rent being paid by your tenant, then you'll make a cash flow loss from the property. In other words, it costs you money to hold the property, and you must come up with the shortfall between the rent and the ongoing costs out of your own pocket. This loss can usually be claimed as a tax deduction by the investor.

The process of borrowing is called 'gearing', and because the outcome here is a negative cash flow, the term negative gearing is used to describe this approach.

According to figures from the Australian Taxation Office, 1.2 million Australians declared negatively geared property investments in 2007–08, claiming total losses of more than $12.75 billion! On average they claimed losses of $10 640 each. Making a 10-grand loss each year doesn't sound like a great investment strategy, so why do so many people do it?

The theory behind negative gearing is that over the long term the capital gain on the property should be more than the total cash paid out while the investment is held, ultimately resulting in a profit for the investor.

Negative gearing is popular because it is reasonably straightforward and, once the property has been purchased, it doesn't take up a lot of time. The ability to claim the cash flow loss as a tax deduction is also an incentive for many investors as it reduces the amount of tax they have to pay. This is especially appealing to high income earners; the higher your tax rate, the more benefit you get from a deduction.

The limitations of negative gearing

While negative gearing is a popular strategy, it does have limitations. The most significant of these is that property prices don't go up all the time. Property prices can and do fall, as seen recently in Australia and around the world with the global financial crisis. History shows that there are usually two to three years of price growth, then one or two years of declines and then three to five years of relatively flat prices. Then the growth phase starts again. The cycle generally lasts around 10 years. This can be seen in figure 1.1, which shows Sydney quarterly median established house prices from 2000 to 2009. Prices rise steadily from 2001 to 2003, then decline in 2004 and 2005. They then stay generally flat until 2009. Graphs from other Australian cities would show similar patterns over time (with differences in the specific timing of the peaks and troughs).

Figure 1.1: Sydney quarterly median established house prices

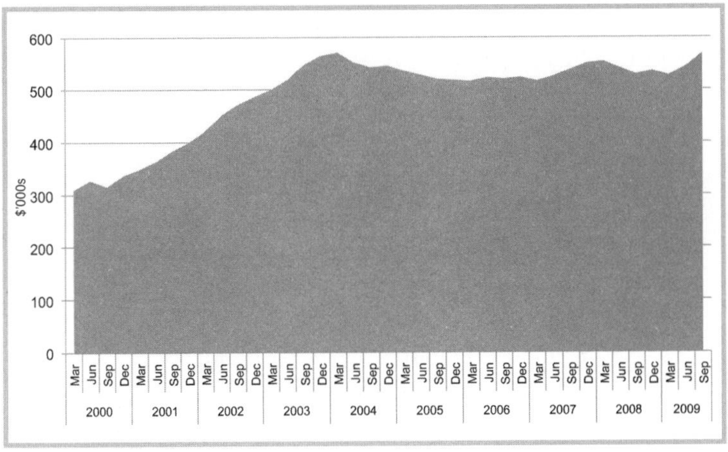

Source: Real Estate Institute of Australia.

13

Another restriction of negative gearing is that because it reduces rather than increases your cash flow, it also reduces your borrowing capacity. The path people often take in real estate investing is to buy one property to benefit from the capital gain and tax deductions, and hold it for a while. Then when they can afford to they may buy a second one, and then possibly a third a few years later. This is the traditional negatively geared buy and hold approach. While it is possible to add to your wealth over the long term (for example, 20 or 30 years), it is a long-term approach to financial freedom.

Interestingly, the Australian Bureau of Statistics once surveyed residential rental property investors and found that 76.4 per cent owned one property, 16.1 per cent owned two and only 7.5 per cent owned three or more.[1] Despite the popularity of negative gearing, three-quarters of all property investors only had one property investment. Why is that?

With negative gearing, the more properties you own the more restricted your borrowing becomes, limiting the number you can purchase. We bet you've never met anybody who owned 14 negatively geared properties.

Negative gearing can also take a long time to bear fruit. When most people say, 'I want to achieve financial freedom', they don't usually mean in 30 years. But figure 1.1 on page 13 shows that if you try to rely on negatively geared deals over a short time frame, there is a reasonable level of risk that you will achieve little or no capital growth, or that the value of your property may even go down in any given 10-year period. This could mean that you pay out money every month on the loan and holding costs for the privilege of losing money in the short term!

(At our seminars we suggest another investment strategy for people who like negative gearing. Send us a cheque for $5000 every six months and claim that as a loss. We'll pocket

---

1   Australian Bureau of Statistics, *Household Investors in Rental Dwellings*, Ref 8711.0, ABS, Canberra, June 1997.

the money, and they can get some of the money back on their tax return … for some reason nobody has taken us up on that offer. Go figure.)

Another problem is the need to fund the monthly loss from other income. Every month you must make the payment on the loan for the property. There are also running costs on the property, such as repairs, rates and insurance. The rental income from the property doesn't cover these in full. So where does the remaining money come from? Straight out of your pocket! This makes it very difficult to achieve financial freedom through negative gearing.

On the road to financial freedom …

You are probably investing with the aim of eventually being able to leave work forever, but negative gearing could mean that you must always have income from your job to maintain your investment.

This will most likely cramp your lifestyle as well; that money has to come from somewhere. Can you afford to fund this gap given your current lifestyle? If not, what are you going to give up? The nights out with friends? The travel? The nice restaurants? Make an honest assessment and have a think about the lifestyle sacrifices you are prepared to make; if they are too great, your investment will not be a success because you won't have the determination to continue paying money out of your pocket to hold the property.

So who is negatively geared buy and hold right for?

Negative gearing might suit you if you enjoy your job and your main investment goal is to make a capital gain over the long term, if you want to be a 'dinner party investor', or if you are seeking to lower your tax bill.

'Dinner party investors' are people whose primary motivation for investing in property is to be able to tell people that they are property investors! You may laugh at this, but there are more people than you think who buy property for this reason. Property investing has become very popular, especially in recent years, and owning a property or two is seen as a sign of wealth and success. If your prime motivation for owning an investment property is to be able to say, 'I own an investment property', well, this strategy is perfect for you. Buy a property and you've met your goal!

If your investment goal is not to leave your job in seven years but rather to make some capital gains over two or three decades, negative gearing may work for you, provided that you choose the properties wisely. Maybe you love your job or you run your own business, are happy to continue working and don't mind the restrictions of negative gearing. Maybe you just want to own a couple of properties that you can sell when you retire, or that will add to your retirement income. This approach could give you a better outcome than not making any investments at all.

Negative gearing also appeals to people who wish to reduce the amount of tax they pay by reducing their income. A negatively geared property will certainly do this because you are paying money out of your pocket every month just to hold the investment, and you are allowed to deduct this loss from other income. By itself, of course, the tax deduction isn't attractive because the investor is still worse off overall; it becomes attractive when it is combined with the expected capital growth of the property. The theory is that overall the investor will make a profit in the long term because the increase in the value of the property will be greater than the total amount paid out over the years to hold the property. Although this is not usually a great path to financial freedom, it does generally work over a long period of time (hence its popularity).

The tax deduction sometimes leads to the flawed thinking that 'The government is helping me pay for it', and so people see this as a clever strategy. But all of the money to fund the investment is coming out of your pocket, and you are making a loss while holding the property. Not having to pay tax on money that you have lost in no way constitutes the 'government helping you' pay for the property. Try sending your next repair bill to the PM and you'll see how much the government helps investors pay for their properties.

Negative gearing might also suit those who want to put in minimal effort. If doing a little bit of research and buying the property is about as much as you want to do and you are happy to hand over management of the property, negatively geared buy and hold may also be an option for you.

On the road to financial freedom...

Negative gearing can work if your goals are modest and long term, but it requires a reasonable income long term to achieve financial freedom with this approach.

Tips for a successful negatively geared buy and hold deal

While negatively geared buy and hold is usually a slow way to achieve financial independence, it might suit your particular needs. Successful investing is all about choosing a strategy that is right for you. So let's have a look at how you can improve your chances of creating a successful negatively geared buy and hold deal. (Many of these tips also apply to the positive cash flow buy and hold strategy, which is discussed in the next chapter.)

Property and location

Generally speaking, buildings such as houses wear out and 'depreciate' in value over time while the land value of the property tends to go up, so look to buy a house that has a large land component. Units and apartments are less likely to appreciate as much as a house on land, and body corporate fees for units and apartments can add significantly to the costs of holding the property. However, if your budget is tight, units or apartments could at least get you in the game.

Buying near the CBD of a major city often offers the best chance of achieving higher long-term capital growth. Properties on the outskirts of a city or in rural areas tend to experience slower growth.

Proximity to infrastructure, industry (jobs), public transport, freeway access and so on are all factors that contribute to the demand for properties in a particular location. The higher the demand the greater the possibility of capital growth.

Getting a better deal

You can improve your chances of profiting from a buy and hold strategy by avoiding paying too much to begin with. One way to help you score 'the deal of the decade' is to improve your negotiation skills. Learn as much as you can about the property, the current market and the area you are buying in, and the type of property you are considering. The more informed you are, the better the price you will be able to negotiate. If you strike a favourable deal on a good property, you will often see a large initial spike in value after you buy, and then a steadier growth over the years.

Managing the investment

Do your homework and choose your rental manager wisely. If you just pull a name out of the *Yellow Pages* you'll get an appropriate reward for your effort. Interview a number of managers, and make them compete for your business. Have them explain exactly how they will manage your property, including finding and vetting new tenants, setting the rent, maintenance and any problems that arise.

On the road to financial freedom...

Always remember that the agent is working for the seller, not for you. When you are buying their job is to push the price up as much as possible; you will be able to combat this if you are well informed.

It is important to delegate, but not abdicate, responsibility for the property. Get everything in writing, so that you can hold the manager accountable. Remember that they might have 1000 properties on their books, so if you don't keep an eye on them your property may not get the attention you would like it to. For example, when finding tenants, property management agencies may send you completed tenant questionnaires for four or five people as a shortlist. An agent that is not diligent may simply give you the first five to apply, which are not necessarily the five best tenants. It's up to you to put in the effort, either to oversee the process or get involved to help ensure that you don't sign up the 'tenant from hell'.

You can choose to manage the property yourself, but be aware of what you are getting into. You will have to deal with the selection process, setting rent, inspections and 5 am phone calls from a tenant who can't change a light globe (don't laugh, it happens!). You might save a little money by not paying a manager, but is it worth it? Serious investors value their time above all else and are prepared to pay for property management, making the process as simple as possible. Managing a property yourself is often not easy, can be time-consuming and is some-times more trouble than it is worth in saved costs.

Achieving maximum rent

While the main focus of a negatively geared buy and hold strategy is long-term capital appreciation, don't forget that you will also be receiving rent, and you should do everything you can to maximise this.

Many landlords make the mistake of viewing the tenant as an inconvenience. Try instead to see your tenant as a valued customer of your property business. Try to find ways to cost-effectively meet their needs. This will allow you to achieve higher rents and also encourage the tenant to stay longer, reducing expensive vacancies.

Here are some suggestions to help achieve emotional buy-in from your tenants:

➤ When they first move in, give them a voucher for the local nursery so that they can buy a plant. Why the nursery? Because if they buy a plant and plant it in the yard this will give them a sense of belonging. Hopefully they will also enjoy caring for the plant and build an emotional attachment to it and their new home.

➤ If you know they don't own a lawn mower, offer to have the grass mown once or twice a month. You might be able to arrange this for $10 per week, and charge the tenant an extra $15 per week for the service. Not only are you endearing yourself to your tenants, you are making an extra $5 per week! You can also do this with pay TV, high-speed internet or a gardener.

➤ Another idea is to offer to install air-conditioning or additional appliances. You could then average the cost out over a year or two and increase the rent accordingly, and ask your tenant to then sign a two-year lease agreement. Putting in air-conditioning might also increase the value of your property.

➤ Buy movie vouchers for your tenants on their birthdays, Christmas or on each anniversary of the lease.

A buy and hold can be ruined by low rents or long vacancies. However, you can't just arbitrarily increase your rent. Do your homework to find out what level of rent is appropriate for your property, and then use strategies such as those given above to win over tenants so that you can command above-average rents.

> **On the road to financial freedom...**
>
> Find out what the market rent is for your property, and then give your tenants a good reason to pay a little more.

A rent that is too high will mean longer vacancy periods, so any short-term gain you might achieve from the higher rent will be erased when it takes you three months to find a new tenant. Strangely, charging a rent that is slightly under market can also be a way to increase profits.

How?

A lower rent can reduce vacancies because your property will be more attractive to tenants. For example, if you rent a property out for $400 per week it might be vacant for three weeks in a year. If you drop the rent to $390 per week, it suddenly becomes more attractive and might only be vacant for one week a year. Let's see the difference in total rent received:

$$\$400 \times 49 = \$19\,600$$
$$\$390 \times 51 = \$19\,890$$

In this example you could actually receive $290 more per year from reducing the rent, because of the shorter vacancy period! There are limits, though; reducing the rent to $7 per week is unlikely to produce a good outcome.

Generally, it's better to find ways to increase the rent by offering your tenants something of value in return, and to use rent reduction only where necessary to combat extended vacancies.

🏠 🏠 🏠

Throughout this book you will read stories of everyday people who have applied various real estate strategies, the lessons they've learned and the profits they have made.

Let's begin by meeting Amanda. She stumbled into a negative gearing deal when she fell in love with a house she was planning to sell and decided to keep it instead. This may have been a good lifestyle outcome, but did it make for a good investment? Let's find out.

Real deal: our retirement home

Hi! My name is Amanda. My partner Matt and I have been together for about 10 years now. We were married late last year and are expecting our first child.

Matt is a carpenter by trade and a registered builder, and he's also been involved in the construction industry. My background is in project management and major event management, and more recently I worked as a real estate sales agent in Queensland, which was a very beneficial experience for our property investing.

I got into property because I was working long hours in my job and didn't want to continue doing this. Matt wanted to work on building projects for himself rather than for other people, and given my management background we thought that between us we had a great combination to give real estate investing a go. I was also attracted by the creative side of renovating properties.

Having a husband as a builder has been a help, but it hasn't been essential to our investing success. While he does work on some of our developments, we try not to involve him too much. This way when the time suits him he can get off the tools too.

Our deal

We were living in Far North Queensland and purchased a cyclone-damaged home in a lovely beachside location with the intention of renovating and then living in the property for a little while before selling it. Well, 'renovating' is a bit of an understatement. There wasn't much of the house left when we bought it, which is why we got it for a very low price. It was a fixer-upper all right! We had to do extensive structural and cosmetic work, which cost us $200 000. We basically gutted the house, installed a new roof (it needed it!), landscaped extensively, added bedrooms and even a swimming pool—the works!

Then we moved in. It was very satisfying and enjoyable living in such a beautiful property that we had created ourselves, and we had a great time and became very emotionally attached to it. It's so beautiful in fact, we thought that it would be nice to spend winters up here during our retirement.

When it came time for us to move out, the house was valued at $700 000, but the global financial crisis was on Australia's doorstep. A property such as this is a lifestyle choice likely to appeal to a smaller number of buyers (probably high income earners), so we expected to get a lower price ($650 000) if we sold with financial turmoil looming. Well, this sealed the deal! We decided to hang onto it rather than sell it as we had originally planned.

The property is now leased and it is negatively geared. The expectation with negative gearing is of course that the outgoing costs to hold the property are more than made up for by the increase in value of the property, but as you can see from the figures below, the value of the property has actually dropped about $50 000 from its peak, so we are actually paying money to make a loss!

We are planning to hold this property for a very long time (we're still a long way from retirement!), so there's plenty of opportunity for things to turn around. Long-term growth forecasts for this area are very good. We expect that by the time we retire properties in this location will be prohibitively expensive, so rather than selling now for $650 000 and having to buy again in 20 years' time at what could be several million dollars we'll just hang onto it.

So we already have our retirement accommodation lined up! For us, this is more of a lifestyle decision than purely an investing one.

On the road to financial freedom...

Even though property prices go up in the long term, this does not mean they are always going up.

The figures

The figures for the deal are shown in table 1.1.

Table 1.1: real deal figures

Purchase price	$190 000
Closing costs	$3 000
Time	Ongoing
Renovation costs	$200 000
Property value (when we moved out)	$700 000
Current value (estimated)	$650 000
Interest and other holding costs (per annum)	$41 000
Rental income (per annum)	$24 000
Cash flow loss (per annum)	**$17 000**

Tips for new investors

My tips for new investors are:

➤ Have a clear plan before you enter into a deal. Thorough research will help you to determine the most profitable way forward.

➤ Learn as much as you can about real estate investing, and surround yourself with experienced investors you can learn from.

➤ Don't overspend on a project just to make it more beautiful. Focus on your profit margin and do only what is required to achieve this.

My current situation

At the moment we have a property in the north-west suburbs of Melbourne, which we are renovating and subdividing. We are fixing up the house to sell it, and putting two units on the rear of the property to sell them off as well. This project is almost complete. We also have another property under contract, where we have submitted plans to the council to build four units on it.

We are now also on the lookout for our next deal, and expect to find something in the next month or two. We are looking for development blocks with a long settlement, so that we have plenty of time to submit plans to the council.

Looking to the future

We have realised through this deal that negative gearing is actually not a good way forward for us. Our Mentor has helped us to establish a clear path ahead, and we are now focused on purchasing properties, adding value and selling them or, rather, developing and selling for a profit. We believe that will increase our wealth more quickly than a negatively geared property. We are trying to focus on building our capital, and plan to purchase a new site every three to six months. We're very excited about this!

According to our plan we are five years away from financial freedom. For us this means having enough positive cash flow from the properties we own that we don't have to work. We don't plan to retire, though. I think we will still continue to develop properties because we enjoy it, but we will be able to take it easy at the same time.

On the road to financial freedom...

Be clear about your purpose in buying a property. If you are not clear on the purpose of your property it will be harder to make unemotional decisions if the property doesn't perform as expected.

🏠 🏠 🏠

While some investors are happy with the results they achieve with negative gearing, Amanda has come to the conclusion that it's not the way for her to meet her financial goals. Although she and her husband are keeping this property more for their retirement than to make money on it, its performance as an investment since they moved out has been disappointing.

In the following chapters you will learn about some more proactive ways to generate profits, rather than just relying on market-driven growth.

Do something!

Think about your goals for the next 12 months and write them down. Then answer the following questions:

- What do you need to have achieved in six months to ensure that you will achieve your 12-month goals?

- What do you need to have achieved in 90 days to ensure that you will achieve your six-month goals?

- What do you need to have achieved in 30 days to ensure that you will achieve your 90-day goals?

- What do you need to have achieved in seven days to ensure that you will achieve your 30-day goals?

And then get started! Address each of the points above and review them regularly. If you're on target, great! Keep going. If not, have an honest look at why you might be falling short and change what needs to be changed.

Bonus content

To hear Amanda discuss her deal in more detail, go to <www.resultsmentoring.com/book1/>.

Chapter 2

Positive cash flow properties

In chapter 1 we looked at buy and hold deals, and this included negative gearing. Maybe you're thinking that this isn't for you. Perhaps you're thinking of something a little faster? While it has its uses, negative gearing is a long-term path.

So what else is there?

Positive cash flow property is just as the name suggests: property investments that *add* to your cash flow rather than *subtract* from it as negative gearing does. It means the investment gives you more 'cash in' than you 'pay out' on the deal. This can be a great way to start down the road to your dreams to reach your *why*.

There are many different ways to generate cash flow through property; in fact, the possibilities are almost endless.

Hands off, cash flow

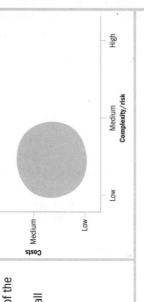

Positive cash flow

(Chart: Y-axis "Costs" labelled High, Medium, Low; X-axis "Complexity/risk" labelled Low, Medium, High)

Cash/equity requirements

- Low/medium amount of money required for a deposit and closing costs

Borrowing capacity requirements

- A low amount of debt will be required, depending upon the price of the property
- Low borrowing capacity requirements because interest costs and all ongoing expenses are offset by the rent

Complexity/risk

- Low complexity, medium risk

Skills requirements

- Medium/high levels of researching, analysis and negotiation skills will be required
- Low/medium level of property investing knowledge will be required

Time requirements

- Medium/high time will be needed to find, negotiate and buy property
- Low time requirement after purchase

Desired outcome

- Long-term cash flow on a low cash deposit

But in this chapter we're going to look at buying a property for which the rent you receive is greater than the costs of holding the investment. This is the simplest form of positive cash flow property.

In this chapter we will feature Jane, who has done quite a bit of positive cash flow investing; however, in this deal she's chosen to buy in New Zealand.

Before we get to Jane's real deal, let's take a brief look at some of the things involved in investing overseas. As you will see in Jane's deal, there can be great opportunities overseas, but each country has its own rules, problems and idiosyncrasies that you must be fully aware of. Investing in another country is not necessarily better or worse than investing at home, but it can be more work and higher risk, so you must decide if you are prepared to take this on.

Buy and hold positive cash flow property

Buy and hold positive cash flow (sometimes referred to as positive gearing) is a straightforward concept: you have more cash coming in (rent) than going out (loan repayments, maintenance, insurance and so on) on the property. You might wonder why anybody would negatively gear a property when it's possible to have positive cash flow, and that's a good question. Some investors get carried away with the tax deductions offered by negative gearing, but the main reason is that positive cash flow properties are more difficult to find. You have to do your homework to find positively geared real estate.

For example, you are unlikely to find positive cash flow properties in major city centres. Most positive cash flow deals are based on finding a low-priced house with a high rental return, and there aren't many of these in prime locations.

On the road to financial freedom...

One formula for finding positive cash flow is to look for a low property price and a high rent. A low price alone is not enough, so research rents and the costs of holding the property as well.

When considering positive cash flow, you are focused on the rental return and not growth in the value of the property. If you happen to get growth, that's a great outcome, but it's not why you are investing into positive cash flow properties. Do not count on high growth in the value of your positive cash flow property.

The extra cash flow will enable you to pay down debt faster too, so as your debt reduces the cash flow increases over time.

Can you reach your goals with buy and hold?

So how do you accumulate wealth over time with positive cash flow buy and hold property? Unlike negative gearing, positive gearing adds to the income you have available. As a basic rule of thumb, banks will count about 70 to 80 per cent of the rent towards servicing debt (the other 20 or 30 per cent is considered to cover the overhead costs for the property such as rates, insurance and maintenance). The extra income can potentially be used to help buy another property because your borrowing capacity may not have diminished (and may even have increased).

Theoretically this approach is unlimited: you could buy as many properties as your available cash will allow. As you pay down your debt, your cash flow increases and so does your ability to borrow to buy more properties. And this cash flow continues for as long as you hold the properties, which can be for the rest of your life. Eventually you could hold enough properties to never have to work again!

The downside of this approach is the number of properties you must buy to replace your income. Let's take a look at an example.

Let's say that you need 20 per cent of the purchase price plus stamp duty to buy a house, so for a $200 000 property it might cost you $50 000 cash to settle (20 per cent of $200 000 = $40 000 deposit, plus $10 000 in stamp duty and closing costs). The amount of cash you get in your pocket from the investment depends on interest rates and the level of gearing, among other things, but let's assume you net around $100 per week from the postive cash flow property. (This means you'd get around $5000 per year net.) That's great! This will help with your next purchase. But in order to buy your next $200 000 property, you will need another $50 000. How long will it take you to save another $50 000 to buy your next $200 000 positive cash flow property?

This extra cash flow is useful but it's not a fast-track to buying another house. And if you're on an income of $100 000, you are going to need 20 of these houses to replace your income ($100 per week by 50 weeks equals $5000 per year, by 20 houses equals $100 000 per annum). If you are on $50 000 you will need 10 of them ($5000 per year by 10 houses equals $50 000 per annum).

On top of that, to buy 10 such properties will cost you $500 000 in deposits and closing costs ($50 000 to buy each house by 10 houses). Do you have $500 000 of lazy cash to buy enough properties to replace your income? No? Most people don't. So it seems that using positive cash flow buy and hold by itself may take you a very long time to reach financial freedom. So what do you do?

To overcome this problem, you might need to try some deals that will provide you with cash lump-sum profits, such as adding value in some way to effect a positive cash flow rental, or maybe do a renovation or subdivision and then sell the property for a profit. This may help you build your cash more quickly.

> **On the road to financial freedom...**
>
> Banks sometimes get nervous about properties in rural or mining towns; they might only lend 60 per cent or 70 per cent of the value of a property (or nothing at all), not the 80 per cent or 90 per cent that you can usually get in the city.

Choosing your strategy

When you first get into real estate investing, it is possible to be overwhelmed by the large number of different strategies you could use. Renovations, subdivisions, buy and hold, developments and many more: which one is the best? Well, the answer is that there is no answer to this question. There is no one *best* real estate investing strategy, but rather a strategy that relates to you and your current circumstances and goals. An approach that is great for one person might be a disaster for another; a strategy that you made a lot of money with might cause big problems for someone else. So it's vital that you take stock of your own situation and make your own decision.

There are a number of different issues you need to consider when deciding what type of deal best suits you:

➤ *Your skill level.* Most novice investors would not be comfortable taking on a large development deal. When you start out, it is safer to take on less sophisticated deals, such as a rental property or a renovation. As your knowledge and experience grow, you can build up to more advanced and—hopefully—more profitable deals. (This will be considered in chapter 3.)

➤ *The time you have available for your investing.* Some strategies are much more time-intensive than others. For example, a renovation will require constant attention and decision making, while a rental property requires only periodic attention. You can assess this by listing your daily, weekly and monthly obligations and commitments on a calendar. The idea is for you to see exactly how many hours you have available to dedicate to achieving financial freedom.

➤ *Your cash/equity position (equity is the difference between the value of an asset and the loan against that asset).* How much cash do you have available to put into this particular deal? This will affect how much you can pay for a property and how much you can spend on the whole deal. You can assess this at any time by:

   △ looking at your bank accounts

   △ getting a real estate agent to value your home(s)

   △ getting current market values for any assets you might own

   △ subtracting all loan amounts, including credit cards.

➤ *Your borrowing capacity.* How much you can borrow will determine how much you can pay for a property. This is based mainly on your income. How much you earn will affect how much you can afford to pay each month to hold the property. This can be established by going to a mortgage broker and simply asking the question 'what's my borrowing capacity?'

➤ *Your risk profile.* It's important to understand the level of risk that you are willing to take on. Are you a bungy jumper or does your sense of adventure peak at a stroll in the botanical gardens? Or put another way, if you were to take $100 to a casino, how much would you bet on black?

➤ *Desired outcome.* Your choice of strategy needs to suit the outcome you seek. Buying a negatively geared property for the rental income will not work as expenses exceed income and market forces alone won't provide enough capital appreciation for financial freedom in the short term.

You probably noticed that some of these issues are related. For example, your income and available cash will affect your borrowing capacity, and if you have more time to devote to your investing you can review more potential deals and improve your skill level more quickly. All of the above must be taken into account, and no one item is more important than any others.

As well as considering your starting position, you must take your financial goals into account:

➤ Do you want lump-sum gains or cash flow from this deal?

➤ Do you want to be hands on or hands off?

And the final thing to take into account is your passions. What are you good at? What do you love doing? Do you like getting your hands dirty? A renovation might be the go. If you don't know the difference between a right- and left-handed screwdriver but you like researching and crunching numbers, a rental property might be an alternative.

This is just an overview of some of the factors to consider when deciding what strategy you should use. Throughout the book we'll explore each of these items in more depth; for example, in the next chapter we'll look at performing a skills assessment to help with your decision. Last but not least, you should also consider the state of the property market: this will be addressed in chapter 4.

On the road to financial freedom...

Take advantage of your strengths and outsource your weaknesses.

Buying property overseas

There are many possible reasons for investing overseas: maybe you are struggling to make profitable investments at home; perhaps you think there are more opportunities overseas; or you just want to be able to make tax-deductible trips to your favourite holiday destination. There is, however, only one valid reason for looking outside your own country to make an investment: *you expect to achieve a higher return on your investment than you can at home*. This is the *only* reason you should look into buying property overseas. Buying property in another country will almost always be riskier, more complicated and more time-consuming, so you must have a good reason for doing so, and that reason is the expectation of a *higher return*. Achieving the same return as you could achieve at home is not good enough, given the increased risk and effort required.

> **On the road to financial freedom…**
>
> Only invest overseas if you expect to achieve a higher return than you could at home.

The property investing opportunities are not necessarily any better or worse in other countries. At the time of writing there are opportunities in the US to buy houses for US$15000 due to the lingering effects of the global financial crisis. You could possibly buy four or five properties for A$100000! These might seem like bargains that are too good to resist, but you must keep in mind that there might be a very good reason for these prices. The US economy is still in the doldrums and it may take many years to fully recover, so opportunities for capital growth may be limited, hence the low prices.

On the road to financial freedom...

If a house is cheap, find out why. You may have found a bargain, or you may have found a lemon.

Things to consider when buying overseas

Here are some things to consider when deciding whether you should invest overseas:

➤ *Tax.* You might have found another country that has lower tax rates than Australia and think that this provides a great opportunity. But this might not be so. When you bring your profits back to Australia, you will most likely be taxed again on the difference between the rates. So, for example, if you pay tax at the marginal rate of 45 per cent and have invested in a country where the tax rate is 30 per cent, you may be taxed a further 15 per cent in Australia.

➤ *Restrictions on foreigners.* Many countries, including Australia, have rules for foreign investment that could stifle your plans. This can include restrictions on buying property and borrowing money.

➤ *Exchange rate risk.* Exchange rates introduce a whole new level of risk. A deal that appears profitable in the local currency could in fact make a loss when you convert back to Australian dollars if the exchange rate has moved against you while you held the property.

➤ *Local knowledge.* A very important part of any real estate investing is getting to know the area you are buying in. As you will see in Jane's deal later in this chapter, this can be overcome if you visit the country regularly (Jane had been holidaying in New Zealand for 20 years) or are an ex-pat.

➤ *Property management.* It can be very difficult to manage a property from another country. And using a management company won't necessarily solve the problem. It will be more difficult to assess potential managers in an unfamiliar country, and standards might generally be lower; for example, it can be very difficult to find a good property manager in the US while living in Australia or New Zealand.

Buying property in New Zealand

The New Zealand environment can be favourable for Australian investors. You can usually borrow money in New Zealand as an Australian resident, and there is no stamp duty, which can result in significant savings getting into a deal.

On the road to financial freedom...

No stamp duty is a bonus when investing in New Zealand, but it's not a reason for investing in New Zealand.

Now we're going to meet Jane. She has found a great little niche for herself investing in New Zealand for positive cash flow. Read on to find out how she did this, and also why positive cash flow is the right strategy for her.

Real deal: positive cash flow in New Zealand

Hello! My name is Jane. I work full time as a head teacher in the Business Services section of TAFE NSW. I'm married with two children, aged 22 and 25, who are full-time university students.

When I was about 12 years old I remember my father and a mate of his deciding to build a house for a bit of extra income. My father worked as a real estate agent at the time so I guess he had some idea of what the market wanted. They built a standard three-bedroom brick veneer home in a bushy area in one of Sydney's northern suburbs. This was in the 1960s when all my friends' houses looked just like ours, which was standard three- or four-bedroom brick veneer! The house sold as soon as they'd finished building it, and I remember the celebratory drinks they had afterwards, so I'm guessing they got a good price. My contribution was to go on the weekends and pass them nails, hammers and anything else they needed. I remember thinking this was quite a fun way to pass the weekend (I loved being outdoors and doing 'tomboy' stuff) and if you made money out of it as well then property had to be a good thing.

My first property deals

My husband and I had been talking for some time about how we would diversify our investments. We've owned some shares for a long time, but we thought there had to be some other ways to create income. It occurred to us that we could afford to get into real estate and that this would be a good way for me to eventually replace my income; I didn't think that shares would do this.

We've holidayed regularly in New Zealand over the last 20 years. We love the country and know it well. One year while there on holiday we decided to have a look at the property market. We found that property prices were much cheaper over there compared with Sydney, where we live.

After making the decision to invest and doing some further investigations, we bought two three-bedroom homes in regional New Zealand which were cash flow positive and very cheap to purchase. These were our first real estate deals. One has had minor cosmetic work done to it (new paint, new heating), the other has had a major renovation including new roofing. Both are rented to stable long-term tenants, and have been good deals for us. However, we had no real idea what we were doing, so the outcomes were more good luck than good management. After finding a Mentor, I was horrified at how we had gone about things; the only saving grace was that both properties were very cheap so if things had gone pear-shaped we wouldn't have lost our life savings.

My latest deal

For my latest deal we purchased a nine-bedroom house in a university town in the South Island of New Zealand (shown in figure 2.1). We had introduced ourselves to numerous real estate agents in New Zealand on our first trip there looking for property, and stayed in regular contact with them. (This is even more important than usual when investing overseas, because it's more difficult to keep up with what's going on in the local market.) This allowed me to get on a number of databases and receive weekly updates from a couple of real estate agents in New Zealand. This deal was on one of their lists.

Figure 2.1: the property

The property was purchased with tenants already in place. All rooms are rented on individual leases: three are on periodic leases and the remaining six are on longer term leases. One of the nice things about most university leases is that students sign up (and pay for) a full year, even though they may go home over the Christmas break. So you are receiving income even as you are able to go in and do maintenance work. (I had also looked at mining towns in Australia, but I was concerned about the mine going belly-up; university towns seem to offer a more stable supply of tenants.)

We had the cash to purchase the property outright, but we chose to use bank finance as we did not want to tie up all our capital. We went for an 80 per cent loan. Our plan for this property is a long-term buy and hold. We aim to pay down the loan as quickly as possible so that we are receiving maximum income from the property.

The rental income is NZ$62 000 per year, and our total holding costs (including rates, loan repayments, repairs, maintenance and insurance) are around NZ$40 000 per year. So we're making a profit of around NZ$22 000 per year!

The figures

My figures for the deal are shown in table 2.1.

Table 2.1: real deal figures

Purchase price	NZ$470 000
Closing costs	NZ$14 000
Holding costs (per annum)	NZ$40 000
Rental income (per annum)	NZ$62 000
Profit (per annum)	**NZ$22 000**

Choosing my strategy

My aim for property investing has always been to eventually replace my income and buy my time back, so that I can leave work when I choose to. This immediately rules out negative gearing. I have never understood the attraction of negative cash flow. I could see that going down that path simply tied you to a job and to the taxman. I wanted to get to a point where passive income from property could replace my job, and negative cash flow didn't do that for me. Positive cash flow property is the best strategy for me in achieving my purpose of replacing income.

My passion in my investing is in crunching the numbers. I have an accounting background, so I'm good with figures. When considering a property, all I consider are the numbers. I don't care at all what the property looks like and I have no attachment to it. I don't think at all about whether I would like to live there. It's just a question of profit.

I often go to property investing network groups and hear people new to investing often have trouble with this. They consider a property based on whether or not they like it or would want to live there, not on whether it will make them a profit. I always tell them: 'Don't buy a property just because it's gorgeous or in a good location, buy it because it will make you money'.

My skills are in managing money and managing people. I currently still work full time while building up my portfolio of positive cash flow properties, and I'm also heavily involved in the community, which is very important to me, so I don't have a lot of spare time. This means that renovating is no good as I don't have the time. The most obvious option is positive cash flow, as it doesn't take up much ongoing time and it allows me to use my skills with numbers. It makes sense for me to work to the strengths that I already have. When I first started in property I thought I could try a renovation, but I quickly learnt that I'm not good at painting or hammering and so this wasn't the right strategy for me. I've learnt to stick to what I know.

Investing overseas

When investing in New Zealand there is of course no language barrier, and there's only a few hours' time difference so that's not really a problem. The biggest difficulty with investing in another country is managing the property. You must have a good team available (such as real estate agents and solicitors) to help you manage your investment. It's taken us a few years to build these relationships, but now that we have it's a great help. We are investing in a university town with a constant supply of students, the people are particularly easy to deal with, and we had no problems opening a bank account there.

A couple of advantages of investing in New Zealand are the absence of stamp duty and the tax deduction we now get on trips over there! The biggest disadvantages are not being 'on the ground', having to rely on your team of people (and it can be difficult to find good property managers in New Zealand) and fluctuations in the exchange rate.

My tips for other investors

My tips for investors looking to start out in property investing are:

➤ Decide on your strategy and area according to your purpose and skills.

➤ Join a group that offers support and mentoring. Make sure the people you are taking guidance from are experienced investors, know what they are talking about and invest successfully.

➤ Never think you know it all—keep educating yourself.

My current situation

I have always felt that as a teacher I have been contributing in a small way to the good of society: I am passionate about education being available to everyone, as a good education gives people choices in their lives. My stable work history and good income mean it is easier to access finance while we are still acquiring a property portfolio. I know some people who became carried away with the idea of property investing full time and threw in their jobs as a result, only to later find they could no longer get finance to buy their next project!

On the road to financial freedom...

Even if you are planning to fund your overseas investments from home, you'll need a local bank account in the other country to handle day-to-day transactions such as receiving rent and paying bills. Talk to a bank in the country you are looking to purchase in and set this up before you start investing there.

Looking to the future

I aim to have matched my income from work within the next 18 months, and I'm on track to do so. I plan to purchase more passive income properties. I particularly like university towns, although I am also looking at regional NSW. Once I have replaced my income I might still work part time, but this will be a choice and not because I have to.

Financial freedom to me means time with my family, time and money to travel, and time and money to set up a charitable foundation.

🏠 🏠 🏠

How's that for a great deal? About NZ$22 000 each year in income. Jane is rightfully very pleased with the outcome. This is a great example of a successful overseas investment. The keys are knowing the country, doing your homework and managing the deal well.

Do something!

Think about your current situation and make an assessment of the following:

- the time you have available for your investing
- your cash/equity position
- your borrowing capacity
- your desire for risk
- your desired outcome: lump-sum cash or cash flow?

Write down your preferences.

Bonus content

You can hear Jane speak about her deal in more detail at <www.resultsmentoring.com/book1/>.

Chapter 3

Positive cash flow properties and add value

In chapter 2 we saw how successful a positive cash flow buy and hold deal can be. Jane is making NZ$22 000 a year from her investment. But if you can think creatively and find the right deal, there is potential to create even more profit by adding value.

Adding value to a deal

Adding value to a deal simply means adding to or improving the property so that its value and/or the amount of rent you receive increases. To do this profitably you must add more in perceived value than actual cost; that is, the expected increase in value must be greater than the outlay required to achieve it.

Hands on, lump-sum cash/equity, with cash flow along the way

Cash/equity requirements

- Low/medium amount of money required for a deposit and closing costs, depending upon property purchase price
- Plus medium/high amount of money required for add-value component

Borrowing capacity requirements

- Low/medium debt level dependent on price of property
- Initially low debt-servicing requirements as interest costs are completely offset by rent until commencement of add-value project
- Debt-servicing requirements may become medium/high if rental income stops during add-value project

Complexity/risk

- Low complexity, low/medium risk for cash flow part of deal
- Medium/high complexity, medium risk for add-value component

Skills requirements

- Medium/high levels of researching, analysis and negotiation skills will be required
- Medium level of project management skills will be required, depending upon complexity of add-value component

Time requirements

- Medium/high time will be needed to find, analyse, negotiate and buy property
- Once purchased, low time will be required to begin with, but increases with complexity of add-value strategy

Desired outcome

- Cash flow coming in while planning for add-value part
- Increased income for long-term hold, or lump-sum cash when sold off once project is complete

Positive cash flow and add value

(Chart axes: vertical axis "Costs" with labels High, Medium, Low; horizontal axis "Complexity/risk" with labels Low, Medium, High)

For example, if you think adding an extra room to a house will increase the value of the property by $60 000, it must cost less than $60 000 to be worth doing. But you must also make a reasonable return on the time, money and effort required.

If your analysis shows that the extra room will cost $57 500 then that's a return of only $2500 for all that effort and time. This probably does not justify the risk. It is of course up to you to decide what level of profit you want to achieve, but a reasonable amount of profit might be $20 000 to $30 000 for adding an extra room. Given this, you would want to be able to add the room for $30 000 to $40 000. Also keep in mind that, even with thorough analysis and research, your expectation for the increased value will only ever be an estimate, so it might be an idea to add a bit extra for a safety margin in case your estimate is a little off.

On the road to financial freedom...

Houses are normally valued by the number of bedrooms rather than the number of living areas. So adding an extra bedroom can be a good way to get an increased rent or selling price.

Multiple income streams

If you have a house with a tenant living in it, you will be receiving one rental payment a month. But what happens if the tenant moves out at short notice, and suddenly you have an unexpected vacancy? During this period you won't receive any rent. That's money you're missing out on. Is there a way to avoid this?

It is possible to find or create deals that will give you more than one rental payment per month. And it's not complicated: you just need more than one tenant! It's possible to have numerous tenants paying you rent through one property. If you own a block of four units, you'll receive four rental payments a month. If you manage and let out your property room by room as shared accommodation, you can generate multiple rental incomes. (There are laws regarding boarding houses, so make sure you find out about these before undertaking such a deal.) If you can build a second dwelling on a block, you'll have two income streams. You may receive more income because you have more tenants paying you rent, and the cash flow will be more secure because it's coming from more than one person. If one of your tenants moves out unexpectedly, you still have some cash flow coming in. Your profit may be reduced until you find a new tenant, but it won't disappear completely.

This is the approach Rachel took in her deal. She purchased a block of four units, which means she receives four separate rental payments a month. This was a deliberate choice because of her circumstances. Rachel was on a low income and she wanted to find a deal that would generate a reliable cash flow for her.

On the road to financial freedom...

The more tenants you have on a property the more income streams you have, which gives you some protection against unexpected vacancies.

Choosing your strategy

In chapter 2 we looked at some of the factors you need to take into account when choosing your strategy. Now let's go through how you might assess the skills you may be able to apply to your next property investing deal.

Skills assessment

A skills assessment means analysing your strengths and weaknesses. If you perform this analysis in relation to your own investing it will help you decide where your strengths are and where you might have problems. All you have to do is identify your strengths and weaknesses, and then analyse the results.

Let's have a look:

> *Strengths.* For example, if you're good at painting and decorating, renovation might be for you. If you are good at managing people, development might be better: you can oversee your team rather than doing the work. If you are good at crunching numbers and research, perhaps positive cash flow is for you.

> *Weaknesses.* What are you *not* good at? What do you try to avoid doing? Answering these questions usually gives people a fair indication of what they feel uncomfortable with and don't enjoy doing. Use this as a guide to help you assess what you might be weak at. Be honest. If you've tried renovating but the house looked worse when you finished, that's probably a good indication of what you shouldn't be doing.

When you read about the many different strategies in this book, consider the options available to you and take into account your strengths and weaknesses.

Again, review the table at the start of each chapter for a summary of strategy needs. If your skills match with the skills for the strategy then this might be where you want to start your investing journey.

As discussed throughout this book, it is extremely important to think carefully about your strategy. It must match your abilities, resources and goals for you to be successful. Everybody's circumstances are different, so there is no one investing strategy that is right for us all. As you read through the deals, take note of the circumstances of each person and what strategy they have chosen, and see how they compare with you and your circumstances.

On the road to financial freedom...

The approach that is right for you can change. Over time you will improve your skills, aim higher with your goals, have more cash available and be seeking different outcomes from your deals.

💰 💰 💰

Now let's meet Rachel. As you will see, Rachel took into account her skills, purpose, passion and experience and decided that positive cash flow property was the way to go for her. And she came across a great deal that allowed her to add value as well.

Real deal: adding value to positive cash flow units

Hi! My name is Rachel. I'm a 23-year-old surfie chick living at home with my mum in coastal NSW. I work as a casual in a surf shop, and I'm also a clown at kids' parties, which I love. But I only earn about $500 per week from these jobs, so I use property to supplement my income.

When I was 17 I heard that 90 per cent of wealthy people either made or kept their wealth in property, so I thought this was something I'd like to try one day. I grew up with a single mum on the pension so we didn't have much money and I don't want to repeat that when I have my own family in the future. Most people go to school, get a job, work for 40 years or so and retire on the pension. Where did all the money go?

It was spent on things that go down in value, such as cars, boats and TVs. This is stuff the people thought they earned or deserved because they've been working so hard. But these things just kept them working. I didn't want to do this. And I don't want to have to work full time, so I'll still have time to help other people.

On the road to financial freedom...

Short-term sacrifices lead to long-term gains. If you can avoid spending money on things you don't really need, you'll reach your financial goals more quickly.

My first property

I bought my first property in 2006 at the age of 19. It's a two-bedroom unit in regional NSW. At that point I didn't think too much about a strategy, I just knew real estate is stable and usually goes up in value so I wanted to own a property. I received a business grant for $10 000 for my clown business and had minimal overheads so that formed part of the deposit, and my mum helped as well. It's currently used as a holiday rental and is 100 metres from the beach and shops. The purchase price was $140 000 with a rental income of $16 000 per annum. I got a 'low doc' loan as my income that year was only $2000 on paper! Interest rates went up to 10 per cent and it was cash flow neutral for a while, then rates fell back to 5 per cent so it's positive cash flow again now. I may sell this property soon as I could get better returns elsewhere.

When I bought it my level of skill was low; I know a little bit more now and would be able to find a better deal. Also it's in my own name, which I now know is not the ideal way to own property.

My second property

Because I don't earn much money from work, I have to invest in real estate using a strategy that will put money in my pocket. I need the properties to pay for themselves and add to my income as well. My investing goal is $50000 per annum in passive income. So for my second real estate investment I again chose positive cash flow as a strategy. Negative gearing makes no sense to me as you lose money every week and become poorer with each property you buy; however, some people are totally sold on it. They may save tax but don't see that they are losing money every week for a possible but not guaranteed future gain.

I had a borrowing capability of $250000 at that point and for stability I wanted multiple streams of income. I decided that an investment in a block of units would provide this: if a tenant moves out you've still got streams of income from the other tenants while one unit is empty. If you buy a house and you have a vacancy period, you don't earn anything at all during this time.

I was searching on the internet when, in the first week, I found a block of units in north-west NSW. It had four two-bedroom units taking up about half of a 1350-square-metre block and it fit my criteria. It was on two titles (so it was already subdivided). This was an unexpected bonus because there was more potential to add value to the deal. The rental income was around $485 per week and there were long-term tenants in place. Some of the tenants have been there since 1983, four years before I was born! I was looking to spend around $250000. The seller was originally asking around $310000, and when I came across the property this had dropped to $280000. I thought this would be a problem, but I managed to negotiate down to $256000, which worked on the numbers for me and so I bought the property.

The property was wrongly listed under single units, so it hadn't attracted much interest and the seller's price expectations had fallen. This was a bit of good luck for me. Also, the property was a bit scruffy, which can turn people off. (But I don't care about this, I just look at the numbers. I'm not going to live there. Sometimes you have to look past the ugliness to see a good deal.)

Since purchasing the property I have increased the rent to $540 per week, by increasing the rent twice by $10 per unit. This is only a small increase per unit but it adds up. The vacancy rate of the town is only 0.4 per cent, and so far I haven't had any tenants leave. When I do have to find new tenants, I think the property will appeal to low-income single people or couples.

I got off to a bit of a rough start with one of the tenants. I went to look at the property after the contract became unconditional. I brought Toblerone chocolate for the tenants to help make a good impression. I knocked on one of the doors and a guy came to answer it. I said, 'Hi, my name's Rachel, what's your name?' He said, 'My name's Shane. What are you selling? I work night shifts and I want to go back to bed'. I said, 'I'm the new owner and here's some chocolate'. I think he was a bit upset. Hopefully things have smoothed over; he's still paying his rent every week.

The other half of the property is vacant at the moment. It's dead flat, and the property is in the middle of town. One possibility I am considering is to put three relocatable houses on the block of land, because I think this will be cheaper and quicker than building.

On the road to financial freedom...

Think outside the box. What creative solutions can you come up with to increase the profitability of your deal?

The figures

My figures for the deal are shown in table 3.1.

Table 3.1: real deal figures

Purchase price	$256 000
Closing costs	$12 000
Initial repairs	$5 000
Time	Buy and hold
Holding costs (per annum)	$23 000
Rental income (per annum)	$28 000
Profit (per annum)	**$5 000**

The bank calculated my borrowing capacity as around $250 000 at that time. I wasn't sure that I would find what I wanted at this price, but the cash flow from this deal certainly helped to increase the amount the bank was willing to lend. I used $32 000 in equity from my unit. I have no personal debt, which helped, and I've shown I can manage money okay.

I could potentially increase the cash flow further by using an interest-only loan. However, I took out a principal and interest loan (rather than interest only), which I felt was the best option for this type of property because I would be paying down the loan from the start. It was the safer option for me and I think the bank liked it better.

I had concerns about whether the bank would agree with the value of the property at $256 000. Also, the loan was almost knocked back several times as there was a chance the property could flood. But I prayed heaps and all the pieces fell into place.

> **On the road to financial freedom...**
>
> A property that generates positive cash flow can help you borrow more, especially if you are on a low income.

My tips for other investors

My tips for investors looking to start out in property are:

➤ take action every day

➤ think positively

➤ never give up.

My current situation

At the moment I'm spending around 15 hours a week on various investment activities. This includes learning about investing, researching and managing my properties. I read heaps of investing books and have learnt a lot of theory, but I also know that I need to take action. My mum has been learning too: she is currently buying her first house!

I also work 25 hours a week at the surf shop, and spend time on my clown business. I go surfing most mornings and study property investing in the middle. I'm extremely blessed.

Looking to the future

For this deal I still need to finalise what I'm going to do with the second block of land.

One of my next steps will be to look at investing in the US. Their market is very depressed and full of opportunities, though I'll have to do heaps of due diligence to buy properties that are high positive cash flow and aren't just cheap lemons. Investing overseas can create more risks if you don't do your homework. I want to get into development projects as well, starting small, then commercial property in the future.

I'm keeping the surf shop job for the short to medium term. I work with a great bunch of people and jobs are hard to come by where I live, and it will still be a little while before my investing allows me to leave work.

When I achieve financial freedom, I want to be able to help people, and that often takes money. I'd love to help people in need whatever that need may be, overseas and in my own neighbourhood.

I want to travel the world. I want to go to France, Italy, Spain, the Greek Islands and Africa. I want to be able to surf a lot, and one day have a family. If it's sunny I'll go to the beach; if not I'll stay home and cook or go to the movies. My future family and I will never have to worry about money. This is what keeps me motivated. I want to achieve financial freedom in the next seven years or less. I'm steadily progressing, taking baby steps most days and big leaps on others. I need an income stream (or gushing river) that does not come from my physical labour. I know real estate will provide this for me, if I work hard and keep learning.

On the road to financial freedom...

Learn to surf. You won't regret it.

🏠 🏠 🏠

You might think that Rachel got lucky finding a deal that was already on two titles and so was perfect for adding value, but that's not the case. Rachel was able to take on this deal because she had done her research, chosen the appropriate strategy and was out there actively searching for deals. That's not luck, that's hard work. And it certainly paid off for Rachel.

On the road to financial freedom...

You make your own luck by taking action.

Do something!

Analyse your strengths and weaknesses. Describe what you are good at and enjoy, and what you would rather not do. Look at your job and what you do on a daily basis. Think about anything that can be applied to property investing; for example, if you are a stay-at-home mum, managing an active family is good experience for managing tradies.

Bonus content

You can hear Rachel speak about her deal in more detail at <www.resultsmentoring.com/book1/>.

Chapter 4

Flips, short-term growth and quick-turn deals

Now we are going to have a look at 'flips', buying for short-term growth and quick-turn deals. Not sure what we are talking about? Read on!

Flips

Flipping, also known as setting up a simultaneous settlement, is a strategy that can be used to make quick cash lump-sum gains. It is a creative strategy and involves significant risks if not done correctly.

Hands on, lump-sum cash/equity

Cash/equity requirements

- Low/medium amount of cash required for deposits and settlements (excluding flips)
- Medium amount of money required each month to service the shortfall between rent and loan repayments (excluding flips)

Borrowing capacity requirements

- As this is likely to be negatively geared (excluding flips) there's a medium borrowing capacity required dependent upon the price of the property

Complexity/risk

- Medium complexity, medium/high risk for lump-sum cash profit

Skills requirements

- A high level of detailed and exhaustive research, area and deal analysis and negotiation skills is required

Time requirements

- Time-intensive for area economic research
- High time needed to find, analyse, negotiate and buy property
- Strategies require a level of attention towards ongoing market analysis during hold period, and/or sourcing of prospective buyer for your flip or quick-turn deal

Desired outcome

- Cash lump-sum profit upon sale of property

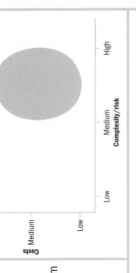

Flips, short-term growth and quick-turn deals

Flipping is actually a very simple process in theory: you buy a property and then on-sell it, for a higher price, to another person before your settlement date. You don't actually have to own a property to sell it, you just need a contract to purchase the property so you can on-sell it before you have completed your own settlement. The key to the strategy is that you organise the settlements to occur on the same day so that you don't actually need finance (as you never hold the property).

Let's see how it's done.

To make a flip work you usually must find a 'bargain' property, so it can take some time to find a good flip deal. Perhaps you can find a vendor who has to sell quickly, or a property that has been on the market for a long time so the vendor has become very negotiable on price.

Once you have found such a property you would attempt to purchase on a long settlement. You then find another buyer during the settlement period, and arrange for the settlement on both deals to occur on the same day. Then, after some lawyers get together and swap contracts, you aim to walk away with a lump-sum profit (because you sold for more than you bought) and your buyer walks away with the keys to the property. Easy! Or is it?

Because you will very briefly be the new owner of the property you must pay stamp duty. Let's look at the consequences of this. If you buy for $100000 you will probably be up for stamp duty and other closing costs of about $5000. You will also have some selling costs on the way out, so allow for legal fees and possibly an agent's selling commission totalling, say, another $5000. You might therefore need to sell at around $120000 if you wanted to make $10000 profit. This is not easy to do in a day so you will need to know your area well and ensure that you can find a buyer who is willing to pay at least 20 per cent more than you did for the same property.

Keys to successful flipping

Let's have a look at some of the keys to success in a flip deal.

➤ You need to find an undervalued property, and this can be difficult, especially if the market is running hot. This means that research is critical to the success of a flip deal.

➤ You need to negotiate enough time in a settlement to secure another buyer. This may mean attempting to negotiate a long settlement period of, say, six to 12 months.

➤ As with any property deal that involves selling, you must find a buyer who is willing to pay a price that will make your deal a success. And to make this even more difficult, you have only a short amount of time to do so.

➤ It is possible to buy a property that needs some simple work done on it. Of course, you would have to negotiate 'access' to the property prior to settlement to complete these works, but this is one way to add value to a property in an effort to achieve your desired sell price. Most vendors won't allow construction during the settlement period, except perhaps landscaping, but it's worth asking.

Risks of flipping

If your success is utterly dependent on finding a second buyer because you don't have the financial resources to complete the deal yourself, you are taking a massive risk with a flip strategy. If you can't find a buyer, you have just bought yourself a whole lot of trouble! For this reason it's essential that you have the ability to actually settle on the property if you have to; that is, having the deposit, stamp duty and borrowing capacity. One way to mitigate this risk is to line up somebody to buy the property from you before you agree to purchase it yourself (easier said than done).

On the road to financial freedom ...

If you structure your flip deal well you can reduce or potentially eliminate the need to obtain finance. But never ever attempt a flip if you are not actually in a position to settle in the event that you cannot find a buyer at the right price.

Let's now move on from deals that require simultaneous settlement to ones that you can on-sell quickly.

A key to the success of these strategies is understanding economic cycles and property market cycles, and knowing what part of the cycle you are in at the time of making your investment, so we'll also look at these cycles and how to stay ahead of them.

Buying for short-term growth

Buying for short-term growth is a quick buy and hold deal where you might hold a property for a short time, rather than indefinitely (as you might with the kinds of deals described in chapters 1 and 2). The aim is to understand the market in your area well enough to anticipate where there is most likely to be rapid growth in property values. You attempt to get in before prices rise, and then cash in your profits by selling once prices go up. In this type of deal you are counting on rapid market growth to achieve your profit.

To succeed with this strategy requires significant research on the economy with particular focus on the city and the local area where you are looking to purchase.

Different pockets or areas behave differently at different times. Some areas will be growing more quickly than others, while some locations might not be growing at all. If you have chosen buying for short-term growth as a strategy, it's your job to get ahead of the game and figure out where prices are about to boom.

There are two useful indicators that can help you with this.

The ripple effect

Some of the most effective areas for buying for short-term growth are areas surrounding a CBD, no matter what city you are in. Typically within any CBD or highly populated area there are geographic features—such as railway lines, freeways, large parks or gardens and rivers—that form the borders of distinct pockets of property.

Let's take a look at Melbourne, for example. There is a pocket west of the city, between the Yarra River, the beach, and the West Gate Freeway (figure 4.1). Within that pocket there are a number of suburbs. Some of these suburbs are more sought-after than others, and therefore each pocket has its own behaviours and traits.

Figure 4.1: Williamstown and surrounds

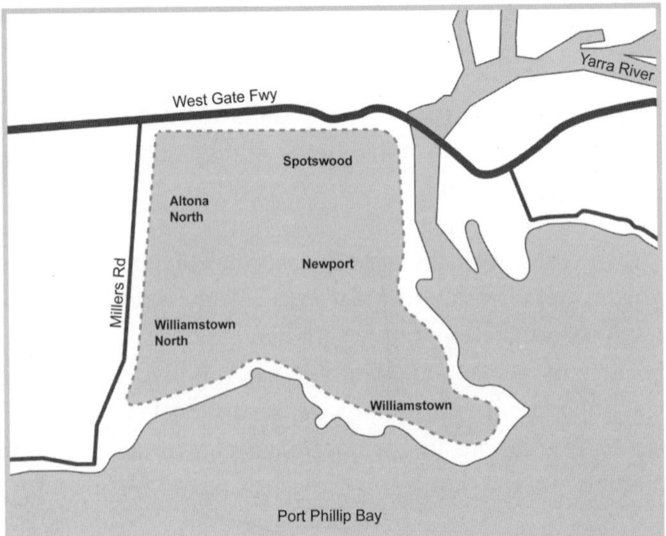

Another pocket in Melbourne is between the beach, the Yarra, the city and major roads leading down to St Kilda (figure 4.2).

Figure 4.2: Middle Park and surrounds

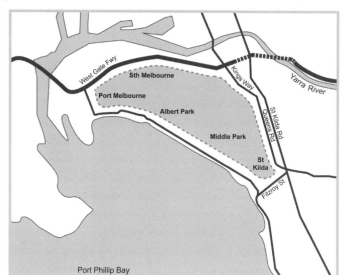

The idea of buying for short-term growth is to know how each pocket behaves; for example, after coming out of a recession the most desirable location in each pocket will likely go up in value first. Let's say in the first pocket we mentioned prices start to rise first in Williamstown; it is by the beach, it is an 'old world' suburb, it is quiet, and yet it is very close to the city. For this example let's assume it is the most desirable suburb in that pocket.

In the second pocket, let's make the assumption that prices will most likely rise first in Middle Park; it is near the beach, close to the city and relatively quiet.

As prices grow in these most highly desired suburbs they become more unreachable for buyers. People will then tend to look for the suburb next to Williamstown or Middle Park to buy into the area. The suburb next to Williamstown is Newport, so in this example Newport may be the next suburb to grow in value. When you hear that Williamstown has grown by, say, 5 per cent and property prices in general are starting to rise, it might be time to buy in Newport if it hasn't started to rise yet and it isn't attracting attention. Then when people start talking about Spotswood it might be time to sell, because this is the next suburb out and growth in Newport might be reaching its peak.

This is an example of the 'ripple effect'. The role of the short-term growth investor is to know and understand the pockets in the city they are in, know which suburbs go up first, how quickly they go up and the rate at which the ripple effect takes hold.

New infrastructure

Infrastructure projects, new major shopping centres, local capital investment or expanding commercial estates are other good indicators that an area might be set for some price growth. For example, if the government is planning to build a new freeway linking a number of suburbs to the CBD, prices in these suburbs are likely to increase because the shorter travel time to the city makes the area more desirable.

Jobs growth in an area means more money flowing into the area and gives more people a reason to live there. So new industries or major employers moving into an area can be a leading indicator of growth to follow in property values. With diligent research you can keep track of such developments and get in ahead of less well informed investors, allowing you to buy at a lower price and then ride the wave of growth as demand increases and homeowners catch on.

You can find out about potential developments in an area from the state planning authorities, local councils and major and local newspapers.

On the road to financial freedom...

Not all investors are prepared to put in the hard yards, so you will be ahead of the game if you put in the effort. Thorough research is usually rewarded.

Considering the economy

Buying for short-term growth is heavily dependent on the economic cycle. It relies heavily on a rising market, so it's vital that you understand the cycles in the economy and can make a reasonable assessment of where things are at.

Let's have a look at a model that might help demonstrate how economic cycles work. Once we've got a bit of a grasp on that, we can relate it back to local property markets.

It might be helpful to think of the economy as having moods. When money is flowing and things are good, we can say that the mood of the economy is optimistic. When things get tight, we can say that the mood of the economy turns pessimistic.

The world economy

In the modern world the economies of most developed countries are linked by the flow of goods and money. This allows countries to sell things they are good at making and buy things they are not so good at making. Cash doesn't move around the world in a steady flow, it moves in waves. And these waves depend on a large number of factors within individual countries, such as the strength of the local economy, government policies and local employment levels.

Because money flows from one country to another, if one has problems this can cause difficulties for others. This was demonstrated to devastating effect recently with the global financial crisis. What began as a local problem in the US with defaults on subprime mortgages started a huge domino effect, and countries, businesses and individuals in all corners of the globe—even those who had never heard of a subprime mortgage—ran into problems as the vast sums of money that usually race around the world slowed to a trickle.

Because of this, many countries (Greece, for example) have been exposed as having way too much debt, and are facing a period of economic 'contraction' as a result. At the same time, Australia had a banking sector with more robust lending policies, higher interest rates that could be dropped to stimulate spending and a strong economy that could slow without falling into recession, and so escaped the GFC relatively unscathed (one of the few countries in the world to do so). This demonstrates that, while interrelated, each country has its own economic cycle.

How the world economy affects local economies

The mood of an economy is related to the amount of cash in that economy. When cash is flowing people have confidence and are happy to spend, but if there's a shortage of cash people become concerned about keeping their jobs, putting food on the table, paying the bills and putting clothes on the kids. Humans have four basic needs for survival (air, shelter, food and water), and when times are tough they revert to 'survival mode'.

Bad times create a negative cycle. As things get tight, people stop spending, which in turn takes more cash out of the economy. For example, if you were considering buying a new car but then things became quiet at your work you might put off buying the car because you are concerned you could lose your job, and so you would rather hang onto that money. If lots of people make the same decision, business at car dealers slows, and then for the same reason employees at the car companies defer their spending because now they are concerned about their jobs. This creates a wave of belt tightening that ripples through the economy.

During such times the central bank of the country will often lower interest rates. This has a significant impact in most developed countries because a high proportion of the population has a mortgage and/or a credit card. Lowering rates puts money back in people's pockets because they don't have to pay as much on their mortgages, credit cards and other loans. This is one of the key factors that gets economies moving again. Prices of many items also drop—or at least increase more slowly—during the bad times as people have less money and businesses compete for the almighty dollar by dropping prices. As a result things start to become more affordable, leading to people spending more. This also helps to start cash flowing again.

Just as the bad times create a negative cycle, the good times create a positive cycle. The people who put off the car purchase when things were looking bad are now more confident in their jobs because business has picked up a bit, so they buy that new car. Car dealers experience a pick-up in business. This in turn gives their staff more confidence in their jobs, and so they are more comfortable spending. Once again the effect ripples through the economy.

On the road to financial freedom ...

Confidence and fear are pivotal factors in economic cycles: when people think tough times are ahead they will close their wallets, taking more money out of the economy and adding to the problem. When good times appear on the horizon, people open their wallets again and start spending, which fuels the good times.

Admittedly the overview above is a little simplistic, but it demonstrates how economies move in cycles. These cycles are unavoidable, given that economies are controlled by humans who have emotions and will look after the basic criteria of life when times get tough: food, shelter and water. In most developed countries around the world, though, there are two institutions that try to exercise some control over the cycles: the government and the central bank.

Factors affecting money supply

Governments can affect the amount of money in the economy through spending policies. By spending on infrastructure the government can inject cash into the economy; during tough times infrastructure projects can be initiated with the specific aim of 'kick-starting' the economy.

We saw this recently in Australia with, among other things, the 'education revolution' programs and the home insulation scheme. The government provided funding for buildings for schools and for individuals to install insulation in their homes. The aim of these programs was to provide work for builders and insulators who were quiet because of the downturn. This has a flow-on effect: as the builders become busy, they have more money to spend and so the cash ripples through the economy. Governments can also spend money on roads, hospitals and other infrastructure projects to provide economic stimulus.

While this process can help the economy, it does take time for projects to get underway. By the time work actually begins, it is possible the economy is starting to turn around already.

A central bank is the independent authority that is responsible for—among other things—setting interest rates. In Australia and New Zealand it is the Reserve Bank, in the US it is the Federal Reserve (often simply called the Fed).

As we've already mentioned, because there are so many homeowners in most developed countries and a high percentage of them have a mortgage, interest rates have a very big effect on an economy. When a central bank recognises a country is in or approaching a recession, they loosen the purse strings by lowering interest rates. This reduces the amount of interest people have to pay on their mortgages, so they have more cash to spend on other things. So rather than ending up in savings accounts at the bank, that money goes out into the economy.

Low interest rates also encourage businesses to spend. Let's say a farmer is considering buying a tractor that costs $100 000. If the farmer needs to finance the purchase at 3 per cent to buy the tractor, that's going to cost him a lot less than if interest rates are at 13 per cent, so he's much more likely to buy if interest rates are lower. When he buys, that money flows into the economy and the people who make tractors get to keep their jobs.

Central banks try to keep the amount of cash in an economy in an appropriate range. Too much cash can be just as much of a problem as too little, because when there's too much cash in an economy prices rise much more quickly, which is not desirable either because it erodes the value of the dollar. The most stable economies are those that are good at managing the cycles to grow their economies at a slow and steady pace.

Property investing and economic cycles

While we have talked about how money flows between countries, let's now have a look at how money flows within countries, from the perspective of the different investment categories of property, shares and cash that will affect your investing. We'll use a model that might help to explain how these categories relate to each other within a country.

As a starting point let's assume we are in the middle of a recession, and have a look at what happens to the economy after that.

During a recession people are in survival mode and their priority is meeting their basic needs of food, water and shelter. Because of this people only buy the basics and don't look to spend so much on luxury items. Under these circumstances the Reserve Bank may reduce interest rates in an effort to stimulate spending and economic confidence. At the same time the government may also initiate handouts or infrastructure programs to inject some cash and activity into the economy.

Given the economic nervousness in the community, people are worried about their jobs and don't want to take on a large debt. People are therefore less likely to want to buy a new home for themselves, let alone invest in property or shares. But people still have to put a roof over their head, so they are more likely to rent. This creates high rental demand and reduces vacancy rates for rental properties. As with any market, high rental demand and low supply will push rental prices up as renters compete for properties and offer to pay more per week to put a roof over their heads.

With the nervousness in the economy, the demand for property falls substantially and therefore property prices generally fall.

This is the starting point in the graph in figure 4.3. (This graph is used for illustration purposes only; economic cycles are neither this smooth nor this regular, but this graph is still a valuable tool for demonstrating how the cycles work.)

Figure 4.3: investing cycles

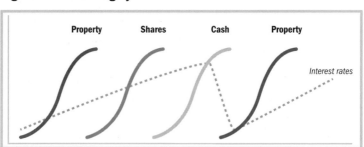

Let's look at the cycles in this graph and how they affect investor behaviour.

The investing cycles

Because rental values are high and prices to buy are low, you can get a good rental yield. Astute investors who are cashed up recognise that money is 'cheap' and returns are good, so they decide it's time to buy real estate. Interest in property starts to increase. There had been an oversupply of houses for sale relative to a very low demand to buy them that led to the low prices, but this now diminishes as properties are bought up. This is the first step in property prices beginning to rise from their lows, but at this time rental rates and interest rates remain static.

Soon people who were nervous about their jobs and about buying start to see a glimmer of hope. The signs of growth in property prices begin to generate confidence, and the people who have sold houses now have some cash to spend. Newspapers are starting to report on positive news in the economy; for example, unemployment may have stopped growing.

Things might still be bad, but now people start to think that they are not going to get any worse. Property prices may have increased but this has happened relatively quietly.

A little further on and people who hadn't noticed the price rises become aware of what's going on. At this stage rents are about the same but property prices are rising, so the rate of return on an investment property starts to drop. This is where the transition to the next phase starts to occur. Astute investors recognise that yields are dropping, but shares are still low after the recession so they start to move out of property and look at the sharemarket.

The community is starting to feel more confident now so people begin to feel comfortable spending; many people think about upgrading to a bigger house and long-term renters begin to think about buying as well. Property purchasers feel they are buying into a growth phase and so are prepared to bid higher at auctions. Soon you won't be able to go to a dinner party or barbeque without somebody asking about your property investing strategy, and then slowly shaking their head because yours isn't as good as theirs.

Newspaper articles now start to appear trumpeting that first homeowners are being priced out of the market by the steadily rising values, and first home buyers who are determined to get in no matter what the price buy at the top of the market. At this point 'speculators' arrive on the scene, thinking, 'I'm not going to miss out. Everybody seems to have an investment property. I'm going to buy one too!' Of course, most astute investors are out of the property market by now, as interest rates are starting to climb.

As we travel along the graph, rental returns have now fallen from their highs to around 2 per cent because of rising property prices. News stories start to appear saying that prices are too high, and people start to lose interest in property because it is becoming unaffordable and returns are lower. This creates a plateau. And not only can people now not afford to buy, but some of the recent buyers may no longer be able to afford to hold with the increased interest rates. Property is losing its allure.

By now the stock market has started to creep up because of the flow of investors out of property and into shares, and news stories start to appear about share price growth. While attention sits squarely on shares, property remains relatively flat.

The casual investor says, 'Hey, the economy is going well, let's go and buy shares because the prices are going up'. As confidence grows the economy begins to move more quickly. In an effort to keep inflation low the Reserve Bank will put up interest rates. But this doesn't stop everyday investors beginning to flood the sharemarket. As sophisticated investors begin to get the feeling that interest rates are peaking we start to see the next transition. The sharemarket is showing signs of overheating because of the flood of new buyers, and astute investors see that they can now get 7 per cent to 8 per cent in a term deposit. Most people just worry about how interest rates affect their mortgage, but clever investors see good returns at the bank for no risk or effort and so start to transfer to cash.

Then something happens. The trigger is different every time, but the sharemarket goes from the latest hot thing to everybody's nightmare as prices tumble and people watch their wealth evaporate. Paralysed by the hope that things will turn around, unprepared investors watch their shares impersonate the *Titanic*, and rather than getting out early with a small loss they get out late with a large one.

People retreat from the sharemarket to lick their wounds and blame their stockbroker. Suddenly everybody wants to be in cash: it's safe and secure. But the astute investor has already been in cash for a while, and so is ahead of the game.

Central banks see doom and gloom on the horizon as pessimism sets in, so they quickly lower interest rates to return money to people. Property prices might fall because people are holding money in the bank and don't want to spend. But once again astute investors are ahead of the game and move back to property as cash deposit rates fall but property rental yields rise.

Can you see where we are now? Astute investors are cashed up. Property prices are low. Interest rates are low. We're back at the start of the cycle! And off we go again…

On the road to financial freedom…

Property is usually the first investment category to grow after a recession. It often leads the economy out of the doldrums.

Based on this cycle you can predict, to an extent, what will happen in the property market. Property prices don't constantly increase. History shows that there are usually one to two years of growth, then three to five years of relatively flat prices, and one or two years of declines. The cycle generally lasts around 10 years. Part of your job as an astute real estate investor is to figure out where we are in the cycle, on both a local and national level, and then use these insights to select a strategy suitable for the current environment. For example, you won't be successful trying to buy for short-term growth in a flat market—there simply won't be much increase in value and you'll be left holding a property in a stagnant market.

Looking at the graph again, it could be argued that it's best to buy real estate in a recession if you are seeking short-term growth, in an environment where governments and local councils are spending money on infrastructure to create growth in the area you are looking at. If you can pick that point you may be able to ride the wave of growth.

On the road to financial freedom...

Don't bet against the market. You will lose.

🏠 🏠 🏠

Matt completed a great quick-turn deal by simply increasing the rent on a property. A quick-turn deal isn't one that relies on settling on the same day nor necessarily on market-driven growth to create profit. A quick-turn deal is one where the investor identifies a problem, quickly and simply solves the problem and re-sells the property. It's a more creative hands-on approach to achieve cash lump-sum gains. It requires some level of wisdom about finding a problem and knowing how to solve it profitably.

Real deal: a quick-turn deal

Hi, I'm Matt. I'm married with three children and have another on the way.

I grew up in Sydney, and my parents had a real estate agency. There was a lot of property talk over the dinner table, and I and my siblings were involved with real estate investing from an early age. Later my older siblings had success in property and became mentors for me.

I got into the building game when my brother took me on as an apprentice; I bought my first property on an apprentice's wage! There was plenty of building work in Sydney, but we wanted to move out of the city and I knew there wouldn't be as much work where we wanted to go, and realised we had to look at other ways to earn an income. That's when we turned our full attention to investing.

The economic environment for this deal

I was looking at the global market in an effort to understand our local market. Times were difficult economically in Australia and around the world, but we felt that there was a high probability of things turning around in the near future and heading up. We felt the property we found and the strategy we chose were just right for the time. The deal was cash flow positive and we thought the market was about to turn up, which was a good way to decrease risk. I see risk reduction as one of my most important jobs as an investor, and we thought the upside for this deal could be quite high and the downside was low.

Our strategy for this deal

We decided to go with this deal because we feel that time is an added risk, especially in the current uncertain world economic environment. The market will go the way it wants to go. I think short-term investments give me more control over the outcome and we wanted to lock in the profits. We also wanted a positively geared property to reduce our risk in case we had to hold long term.

Our deal

My strength has been buying a block of units and then selling them off individually. I made an offer on a property for one of these deals and was rejected, but the agent got an idea of what I was after and so brought me another property to consider. It was a six-unit property that I wasn't initially attracted to, because I had concerns about the fire ratings and if it would be able to be strata titled as it wasn't the typical construction we had been dealing with. To me it wasn't worth the risk and effort of the deal, but I started to think about what else I could do with this property.

At a rate of 10 per cent the rental return was fairly attractive. After brainstorming ideas with my Mentor, I asked the agent if he thought the current rent being paid on the units was market value, and he said no, the rental rates were 10 years old. That's when a light went on and I saw an opportunity.

The units were very basic and nothing special to look at, and the kitchens were from the 1970s and hadn't had any work done on them. But this didn't matter for the type of deal we were now considering. We saw an opportunity to increase the rent to market value and so sell the property at a higher price, and still be able to offer our purchaser a 10 per cent return.

We initially offered $195 000, and actually thought we had secured the property at this price. But before we signed the contracts another buyer came in and pushed up the price. We increased our offer on the condition that the rent in one of the properties was increased. We secured the property for $225 000, so each unit cost us around $40 000, which was still very cheap. With this strategy in mind, I think we could see the potential in this property more than the other buyer could, so we were prepared to pay a higher price. Paying $30 000 more than we had planned was the only real speed bump in this project.

On the road to financial freedom...

Being well prepared and knowing your numbers thoroughly may mean you are willing to pay more for a property than other investors, if you can see profit potential that they can't.

We wanted to put the rent up, but we didn't want to do the wrong thing by the tenants, so we spoke to them before buying the property. We wanted to add some things to the units so that they felt they were getting value for the rental increase, so we added some fly screens and other things that the tenants asked for.

The original rental income was around $80 per unit per week, but by spending only $1300 on the property we managed to increase the rent to $110 per unit, which was market rent at the time. This meant we were able to increase the rent from a total of $480 to $660 per week. There was nothing else in the area that was only $80 per week, so we felt quite comfortable with the increase.

We then put the property back on the market, and ended up selling for $365000.

We felt that this was a straightforward deal as the market told us before going in that what we wanted to do was achievable. We earned rent while we held the property, and then made a good profit on the sale. We could have held onto the property for the long term and made a good return from the rent, but at the time our aim was to make short-term lump-sum gains to quickly increase our capital. This is one of the quickest deals we have done.

We were very pleased with the result.

The figures

You can see from the figures in table 4.1 (overleaf) that this was a pretty good deal for us! We achieved a great return without a high dollar input.

Table 4.1: real deal figures

Purchase price	$225 000
Closing costs	$16 000
Project length	3 months
Holding costs	$6 725
Improvement costs	$1 300
Rental income	$5 900
Sale price	$365 000
Sale costs	$13 875
Profit	**$108 000**

Yes, that's right. We made $108 000 in three months, just by increasing the rent! We knew and understood the economic environment at the time, we knew the market and current rental values. I think it's safe to say we chose the right strategy for the market. We are very proud of this deal.

Tips for new investors

My tips for new investors are:

➤ Having a mentor is a great form of insurance.

➤ There's always a deal out there that will suit the current economic conditions. If you look in the right areas relative to the conditions you can find a great deal.

➤ Know why you are investing in a particular area and become an expert in that area.

➤ Become an expert in your chosen strategy and the numbers behind the strategy.

My current situation

I was a full-time builder for around 10 years, but these days I prefer to be making the deals rather than doing the physical work. I'm now a full-time investor in real estate and the share-market, with the assistance of my wife.

Looking to the future

My wife and I plan to keep building the property side of our investments. We see potential deals all the time, but of course our finances can only stretch so far and we can't do them all, as much as we might like to. So now we are looking for business partners and are planning to expand that way.

Our ultimate goal is to home-school the kids and be able to do a lot of travelling. That's what financial freedom would mean to us. Property has already helped us do a lot of travelling, and once we are on the road we don't really want to come back, so to travel more is one of our big desires.

We still have a way to go to reach financial freedom, but we think we are making good progress and we are excited about the future ahead.

🏠 🏠 🏠

Matt made $108 000 in three months — what a great deal! When choosing a strategy Matt took note of the current economic environment and how this would affect his deal, became an expert in the area he was looking in and thoroughly understood the numbers in his deal. This allowed him to see an opportunity that other investors missed.

Do something!

Using the method outlined in this chapter, make an assessment of what stage you think we are currently at in the investment cycle and write this down. Do some research and back up your conclusion. Take a few weeks if needed to do some thorough investigating. How does this info affect your investing decisions?

Bonus content

To hear Matt speak about his deal in more detail, go to <www.resultsmentoring.com/book1/>.

Part II

Renovations

Chapter 5

Live-in cosmetic renovations

You've probably seen renovation shows on TV: it seems like it might be fun, and an easy way to make some money. And if you like painting and decorating, you can even do some of the work yourself. How hard can it be? Buy a 'renovator's delight', splash a bit of paint here, put in new appliances there, a few trips to Bunnings, and then sell it for a big profit. Right?

Well, it's not actually that simple. If you get carried away with a renovation and go into it thinking it will be fun and exciting, you might end up with an expensive property that nobody wants to buy, even though you think it looks beautiful. Cost blowouts, schedule blowouts, emotional blowouts—an ill-conceived reno can leave you wishing you had just left your money in the bank.

Hands on, lump-sum cash/equity

Cash/equity requirements

- Low/medium amount of money required for a deposit and closing costs, depending upon property purchase price
- Low/medium amount of additional money required each month to fund the reno

Borrowing capacity requirements

- Low/medium amount of borrowing will be required, dependent upon the price of the property
- Low amount of additional money needed to service debt as you are living in the property

Complexity/risk

- Low/medium complexity, low/medium risk for lump-sum cash profit
- Easy fallback strategy: if you overcapitalise you can live there for longer

Skills requirements

- Medium levels of researching, area and deal analysis and negotiation skills will be required
- Medium levels of project management and people skills will be required
- Medium handyman skills if DIY

Time requirements

- Medium time needed to find, analyse, negotiate and buy property
- Medium/high time required to execute the reno at home, dependent upon time frame allowed to complete reno

Desired outcome

- Cash lump-sum profit upon sale of property

Live-in cosmetic reno

Costs: High / Medium / Low

Complexity/risk: Low / Medium / High

Renovating a property that you are living in can be a great way to get started in property. If the improvements are largely cosmetic — such as painting, new carpet, appliances, taps — it can also be a fairly cheap way to add value to a property (as you will discover, Gladys renovated her unit for only $8500). Avoiding structural work — such as re-roofing, re-stumping and extensions — will help to keep costs down. This also means that you don't have to get the council involved as you do not require building or planning permits. And living in the property while the project is underway means that you are only paying for one property, instead of paying the costs of your own home and the holding costs on your investment property. This is a great money saver (though it does require some lifestyle sacrifices).

On the road to financial freedom...

The key to successful renovating is to add more in perceived value than actual cost.

If you have never owned a property before then you might qualify for the First Home Owner Grant, which could help reduce the amount of your own cash that you need to get into the property. (There are rules about who is eligible for this, so don't just assume that you will get it. Refer to your relevant state government website for details.)

The key to success with any reno deal is to add more perceived value than actual cost. This means that the cost of any improvement you make to the property must be less than the resulting increase in value of the property. For example, you might calculate that refurbishing the kitchen with new cupboards, shelves and appliances will add $20000 to the selling price of the property, and it will cost you $10000 to do the work. So refurbishing the kitchen will earn you $10000 and may be worth doing. If it was going to cost you $20000 to redo the kitchen, it would not be worth doing. While it might make the house more attractive, the increase in value wouldn't justify the expense.

> **On the road to financial freedom...**
>
> People often think renovating is a good option because they can do the work themselves, but keep in mind that if you are spending your time hammering and sawing you are not out finding deals. What's the best use of your time?

Rent it or sell it?

There are two common reasons for doing a reno: you want to either sell it for a profit or increase the rent. Let's have a look at the two different options.

Buy–reno–sell

Renovating to sell can provide a solid return in a short amount of time. Projects can last six months, or even less, and at the end of the project the profit is fully realised and can immediately be put to use in the next project. Undertaking successively larger reno projects, or multiple projects simultaneously, can help you to build capital more rapidly. In fact, people can make a career out of doing this. You can repeat the process until you decide that you have enough cash to begin to buy assets that will generate a passive income for you.

The buy–reno–sell strategy represents the most aggressive approach to making money through renovation. It aims to extract every possible cent out of the property as quickly as possible, for the purpose of reusing the proceeds to create more profit in the next deal.

Buy–reno–rent

Buy–reno–rent is less common, and usually involves a less expensive and less detailed reno than buy–reno–sell. Buy–reno–rent is similar to a buy and hold, but it's a little more aggressive because you are investing money to create more value in the deal, rather than just holding and hoping that the value of the property will increase over time.

Investors who renovate a property to rent it out are aiming to generate income by receiving rental payments, rather than receiving an immediate lump-sum cash profit. The benefit of the renovation is that a higher rent can be charged because the property has greater appeal to tenants. The renovation is also likely to result in a higher selling price when the property is eventually sold. In addition, the added value may give the investor some equity to draw upon in the meantime. This may get you to your goals more quickly because you are buying the next property in less time, but keep in mind that it does come with added costs and risks.

Renovating to rent can also be a good way for novice investors to get into the rental game by buying a slightly cheaper property that needs some work, and slowly renovating it over time as personal finances allow, and increasing the rent on the way.

With a buy–reno–rent investment the renovation should focus on creating a low-maintenance property that is suitable for the demands of the rental market. It can be a good idea to renovate in a way that is easy to touch-up and refresh between tenants.

On the road to financial freedom…

Both renovating to rent and renovating to sell can produce good results. Decide what your goals are for your project and then choose the appropriate approach for you.

Which option is best for you depends upon the outcome you seek, and there are good arguments for either choice. As with all strategy decisions, consider your goals and circumstances and make an informed decision based on the numbers.

🏠 🏠 🏠

Now we're going to meet Gladys, who is going to tell us about how she overcame the added difficulty of having English as a second language to become involved in real estate investing.

Real deal: my first deal

My name is Gladys. I live in Sydney, and I've been living in Australia for about 14 years. My English isn't the best. I'm a single parent with a 12-year-old daughter (she is a really, really great girl), and I also take in foster children. I only had $6000 in savings when I decided to look into property investing.

Before I started property investing, I was trying all different kinds of jobs, anything that would give me the flexibility to look after my child and give me time for investing. I heard stories about people making money with property so I started reading books about investing in property. I didn't have any kind of experience in property or investing but I was keen to learn. As I started to learn about property through books and a real estate mentoring program, I decided that because of my small budget cosmetic renovation would be a good strategy for me.

The deal I eventually did was a live-in renovation that took eight months. Living in the property while renovating saves costs because I didn't have to pay for two properties at once — the investment property and a house for me to live in.

Finding the property

I decided that I needed to find a property that wasn't too far away, and that was close to good amenities. I searched on the internet, talked to real estate agents, walked the streets of the areas I chose, and kept an eye on what was for sale. The property that I found was listed on a website in a new area I had started to look in. It was a unit on the top level of the building, and there was a communal laundry with only one washing machine to share between six units. It was in good condition. I was very nervous when making the deal, but I went ahead anyway.

On the road to financial freedom...

The way to overcome anxiety is to create confidence. The way to create confidence is through knowledge.

The reno

The property was partly renovated before I bought it, so I only had to do a cosmetic renovation: painting, changing the kitchen benchtop, putting in a new cooktop, adding an internal laundry and scrubbing a bathroom. I was renovating thinking of the next possible buyer. Initially I thought it would be for a first home buyer (so I would have changed the carpet and all the bathroom and kitchen taps and put in new light switches), but then with the market changing it was renovated for an investor (so I just cleaned everything, and didn't need to put in new things such as taps). The addition of an internal laundry was very important to make the unit more appealing to the next buyer.

Figure 5.1 (overleaf) shows some pictures of the property after the renovation was finished.

Figure 5.1: renovated property

I had problems because this was my first deal. I didn't know how to find good tradies or where to shop for materials. I ended up contacting three tradies and chose the best one, and I now shop for material at hardware stores and auction houses. I also didn't know what colour to paint, and things like that. But when I asked my Property Mentor he helped me figure out that these decisions needed to be based on what my target market would want. I also had difficulties because English is my second language. Property investing can be complicated, and sometimes I had trouble understanding what was being said to me. However, I got better as I went along, and there were always people to help me when I needed it.

The figures

Because I was going to live in the property for at least six months, I was able to apply for the First Home Owner Grant. This money went towards stamp duty, which is why my closing costs were low. My figures for the deal are shown in table 5.1.

This was a great outcome for me and I was very excited about it. The most important part for me was to get in and out of this deal while the interest rates were still low, which I managed to do. Everything went as I planned because of the good help of my Property Mentor.

Table 5.1: real deal figures

Purchase price	$320 000
Closing costs	$5 900
Length of project	8 months
Holding costs	$16 500
Reno costs	$8 500
Selling costs	$11 700
Sale price	$390 000
Profit	**$41 400**
	(including $14 000 First Home Owner Grant)

On the road to financial freedom...

When deciding what to include in your renovation, always concentrate on the needs of your target market. Use neutral colours that are likely to appeal to the broadest group and avoid imposing your personal tastes on the property.

Marketing and staging the property

I found a good buyer for the property because the advertisement was designed for the target market, and as such it generated a lot of interest. My Property Mentor gave me a lot of help with the ad.

I also staged the unit for sale, made the place look as tidy as possible and took personal items out of the property. I decluttered and made everything look very clean, and got rid of rubbish. I bought new towels and soap for the bathroom, and new tea towels and coffee cups for the kitchen. Cushions were placed in the lounge room and there were new covers for the beds. I think this all made the property brighter and increased the appeal to buyers.

Tips for new investors

My tips for investors starting out in property investing are:

➤ have money for the deposit

➤ save as much money as you can to cover all the costs

➤ keep on taking action.

On the road to financial freedom...

In your first cosmetic reno deals you might want to target a six-month turnaround. As you get more skilled, you will be able to get this down to much less than that.

My current situation

At the moment I am working as a foster carer and I just completed my first deal. I try to spend three or four hours each day on my investing. I am back renting again while I look for the next deal.

Looking to the future

My goal is that I would like to change my lifestyle. I would like to have the freedom to not worry about extra expenses. I would like to enjoy good times with my daughter and also be able to give her a good education, and have the opportunity to have some time with my family who I haven't seen for a long time. I still would like to do foster care but it would be a bit different then, without much pressure. I would like to have my home open for everyone (well, for almost everyone!).

Another strategy I would like to try for the future is sub-division. I will also keep on going with the program to get the support when buying and selling the next investment property. I expect to achieve financial freedom in 10 years' time, or hopefully sooner.

🏠 🏠 🏠

As you can see, a live-in cosmetic reno can provide a great outcome, even for inexperienced investors.

Do something!

Take some time to review the homework you have already done and compare your responses to the strategy details at the start of each chapter. At this point, which strategy appeals to you most? Why?

Bonus content

To hear Gladys speak about her deal in more detail, go to <www.resultsmentoring.com/book1/>.

Chapter 6

Cosmetic renovations

A cosmetic renovation can be a great way to add value to a property without putting in too much time, money or effort. If you limit your improvements to things like painting, installing new doors and putting in new carpet, your deal will be much more straightforward than if you start adding rooms, removing walls and building extensions.

In this chapter we are going to look at some number crunching you can do to help find and buy a reno deal, and then we'll hear from Troy S about his cosmetic renovation project.

Hands on, lump-sum cash/equity

Unit — cosmetic reno

Cash/equity requirements

■ Typically low/medium amount of money required for a deposit and settlement costs

■ Low/medium amount of additional money required to fund the cosmetic reno

■ Medium amount of ongoing cash required to service the debt of the vacant property

Borrowing capacity requirements

■ Typically low/medium debt-servicing requirements relative to other strategies, dependent upon the price of the property

Complexity/risk

■ Low complexity, low/medium risk for lump-sum cash profit for an add-value project

Skills requirements

■ High levels of researching, due diligence, area and deal analysis and negotiation skills are required

■ Medium levels of handyman skills if DIY

■ Medium project management and people skills required

Time requirements

■ Medium amount of time required to find, analyse, negotiate and buy property

■ Medium/high amount of time required to execute the reno (highest if DIY)

■ Typical time frame for cosmetic reno project is six to nine months

Desired outcome

■ Cash lump-sum profit or equity gain

100

It's all about the numbers, not the dwelling

A successful renovation deal is about creating more in perceived value than the actual cost of the improvements to the property. The profit from a renovation deal doesn't just depend on what colour you paint the bedrooms, what appliances you put in the kitchen and the tiles you put in the bathroom. It's possible to create a beautiful house but still have an unsuccessful deal if you haven't delivered what the market wants. (You'll read more about this in chapter 7.)

The profit on any good property investment is determined *before you buy the property*. Before you start looking, you must establish the figures and parameters for the project that will make it a success for you. Once you have done this, finding the property will boil down to a simple question:

Does this house match my criteria? No. Don't buy it!

Does *this* house? Yes. Buy it!

It's not just a case of looking at the house to imagine how beautiful it could be when it's finished but understanding the numbers to assess the profit you could make in the deal. You must make business decisions; you are trying to make money.

To simply decide that you want to do a reno and then hunt around for a property that needs work is a very risky approach. Ideally you must have a good reason for choosing Renovation as your strategy, have done your numbers and carefully researched areas where you believe you are able to find a deal that could produce the profit you need to achieve.

On the road to financial freedom...

Cosmetic renovations can provide deals with a low entry price and short turnaround, which can be great for beginners.

Quick reno deal analysis

Two critical factors in any property deal that involves on-selling to make a profit are:

➤ how much you pay for the property (the 'purchase price')

➤ how much you can sell it for.

The price you pay for the property is within your control insofar as you can negotiate a price that makes financial sense or choose to walk away. However, it is difficult to know with absolute certainty what you will be able to sell it for. You can get an idea of a realistic end sale price by talking to real estate agents and researching recent sales of similar renovated properties in the area.

A simple formula that can quickly help you assess the potential of a cosmetic reno deal is:

desired selling price = purchase price × 133%

What this means is that you need to confirm that your renovated property is likely to sell for 33 per cent more than you bought it for. This 'mark up' of 33 per cent is based on the assumptions shown in table 6.1.

So how do you use this calculation? Let's assume you're inspecting a potential renovation deal that is listed for sale at $200 000. If you multiply $200 000 by 133 per cent, you'll get a desired selling price of $266 000.

You then need to determine if $266 000 is a realistic selling price for your property once it is renovated. The first step in doing this might be to simply ask real estate agents for their opinion. Keep in mind though that some agents may exaggerate the value of the renovated property, anticipating that this might be what you want to hear. Therefore the next step is to do some research of your own. To do this it would be valuable to find some recent comparable sales in the area. You can purchase useful house price data from online services such as Australian

Property Monitors and RPData, and study recent auction results. If you establish a good relationship with real estate agents in the area, they might be willing to provide you with some figures of recent sales in the area for free.

Table 6.1: 33 per cent 'mark up'

	Unrenovated purchase price
For closing costs (stamp duty, bank and legal fees and so on)*	+ 5%
For holding costs (interest, rates, utilities and so on for six months)**	+ 4%
For renovation costs	+ 10%
For profit [†]	+ 10%
For selling costs (agents' fees and legal fees)[††]	+ 4%
	= 33%

* Typically 5 per cent of the purchase price will be sufficient to cover the closing costs of a property in Australia. In New Zealand this is much less.

** This assumes that you are holding the property for six months at a rate of 8 per cent interest, with a loan for 80 per cent of the value of the property.

[†] This is just a guide; you can use a different profit figure if you wish and adjust the calculations accordingly.

[††] Typically 4 per cent of the purchase price will be sufficient to cover the selling costs of a cosmetically renovated property.

You can use these figures to assess whether the property you are looking at has the potential to sell for $266000 or more. For example, if similar renovated properties have only been selling in the area for $240000 or less, this deal might be one to avoid. If your research shows that this figure is likely to be $270000 or higher, you might have found a deal that warrants further investigation!

There are three things you must keep in mind with this analysis.

First, this ratio is just a guide. It only provides you with an initial idea of whether a deal has potential. It is not a substitute for extensive research and analysis.

Second, the sales prices you obtain in your research must be for very similar properties. No two properties are exactly alike, but you have to compare properties that at least have the same number of bedrooms, bathrooms, living areas and car spaces, and are on a similar sized block in the same condition. Are they roughly the same age as the property you are looking at? Have they been similarly renovated? Will they appeal to the same type of buyer? If you are calculating a possible selling price based on properties that are not similar to yours, your analysis is useless.

Third, the formula relies on the reno being done for around 10 per cent of the purchase price. Therefore sticking to a reno budget becomes critical. It's a good idea to research the reno costs to ensure this is possible.

In chapter 7 we'll examine how you can use these figures to find areas with good potential for renovation deals, but now let's get into how much cash you need to make a deal work.

How much money do you need to buy and renovate a property?

Continuing with the above example, if you are going to buy a property for $200 000 for the purposes of renovating, how much cash do you need at the start of the deal? Let's have a look.

If we assume you are borrowing 80 per cent of the purchase price of the property and use the percentages from the table on page 103, we come up with the figures shown in table 6.2.

Table 6.2: money needed at the start of the deal (80 per cent loan)

	Cost	% of purchase price	Cash required (80% loan)	% of purchase price
Purchase price	$200 000	100%	$40 000*	20%
Closing costs	$10 000	5%	$10 000	5%
Holding costs	$8 000	4%	$8 000	4%
Renovation	$20 000	10%	$20 000	10%
Profit	$20 000	10%	–	–
Selling costs	$8 000	4%	–	–
Sale price	$266 000	–	–	–
Total	**–**	**133%**	**$78 000**	**39%**

* A deposit of 20% of $200 000 equals $40 000.

Obviously your profit isn't a cost, and the selling costs are covered from the proceeds of the sale so they don't need to be included at this stage. So we can see that as a rough guide you might need about $78 000 to purchase and renovate a $200 000 property with an 80 per cent loan. This is roughly 39 per cent of the purchase price; to give a little bit of margin for error we suggest that you use 40 per cent, which in this case means you'll need about $80 000.

What happens if you don't have $80 000 in cash or available equity? Well, you have a few choices. Firstly you can look in cheaper areas or at a cheaper style of property. But if you are really keen on a particular property that is $200 000, you may be able to increase your loan-to-valuation ratio (that is, borrow a greater portion of the purchase price) in order to reduce the amount of your own cash needed.

On the road to financial freedom...

The loan-to-valuation ratio (LVR) is the percentage of the price of the property that you borrow. If a property costs $100 000 and you borrow $50 000, your LVR is 50 per cent. If a property costs $100 000 and you borrow $80 000, your LVR is 80 per cent.

If you have your finances in order you may be able to obtain up to a 95 per cent LVR loan to purchase an investment property. This may mean that you don't need as much cash up front to finance the deal, although there is one extra cost: lenders mortgage insurance (lenders mortgage insurance is a fee charged by most lenders when the LVR exceeds 80 per cent). Let's compare the figures with a 95 per cent loan (table 6.3).

Table 6.3: money needed at the start of the deal (80 per cent loan compared with 95 per cent loan)

	Cost	Cash required (80% loan)	Cash required (95% loan)
Purchase price	$200 000	$40 000	$10 000
Closing costs	$10 000	$10 000	$13 000[*]
Holding costs	$8 000	$8 000	$9 000[**]
Renovation	$20 000	$20 000	$20 000
Profit	$20 000	—	—
Selling costs	$8 000	—	—
Sale price	$266 000	—	—
Total	**—**	**$78 000**	**$52 000**

[**] This is higher because of lenders mortgage insurance.
[**] This is higher because of the increased interest payable on the amount borrowed.

You can see that taking out a 95 per cent loan has reduced the upfront cash requirement by around $26 000, and you now only require about 25 to 26 per cent of the purchase price up front. Of course this hasn't reduced the cost of the deal overall because you have to pay that extra money back to your lender, but it does reduce the amount of cash required up front.

Even if you do have the $78 000 (or $80 000) required up front, you could still take out the higher LVR loan to give you more cash to do the reno, but of course you must have a good reason for doing so. And what's the *only* good reason for doing so? You believe spending more on the reno will give you an increase in your profit that makes the extra expense worthwhile.

However, a higher LVR increases the risk in any deal because you are taking on more debt. It may also mean a lower profit due to the extra costs of lenders mortgage insurance and the interest on the extra borrowed amount. The higher LVR can also make it more difficult for you to take out additional loans to buy other properties, as the banks will see you as an increased risk while currently holding the property. As always, do your numbers to see what will produce the best result for you.

On the road to financial freedom...

Lenders mortgage insurance (LMI) protects the lender, not you (even though you have to pay for it), so don't think that you have protection if you can't make a payment.

Let's now turn this equation around and look at it from the other end so that you might be able to determine the value of the property that you can afford to take on and complete comfortably. If you recall, you looked at your financial position (chapter 1) given the amount of cash you have available.

Let's say you have $120 000 in cash and/or available equity to spend on a property deal. You have considered your circumstances, your strengths and weaknesses, how much time you have available and the level of risk you are prepared to take on. From this you have concluded that a cosmetic renovation is a good strategy for you.

We saw above that with an 80 per cent loan you need to have about 40 per cent of the purchase price up front. So, if you have $120 000 cash to spend, you can work out how much you can afford to pay for your unrenovated property as follows:

$$\$120\,000 \div 40\% = \$300\,000$$

This tells us that you can afford to pay about $300 000 for a property to cosmetically renovate and sell within a six-month period.

What about if you want to take out a 95 per cent loan? We know that a 95 per cent LVR means you must have about 25 per cent of the purchase cost up front, so:

$$\$120\,000 \div 25\% = \$480\,000$$

So taking on the higher risk of a 95 per cent loan in this example means you could afford to buy a property for $480 000 instead of $300 000. This doesn't mean you *should* do this, just that it's an option.

Using the numbers to find your property

Everything that we've done above is designed to help you begin looking for a potential deal.

Let's say you have $120 000 for a reno deal but don't know where to start looking. You know that if you have $120 000 you can buy a property for around $300 000 on an 80 per cent LVR. And if you buy it for around $300 000 you need to be able to sell it for around $400 000 ($300 000 × 133% = $400 000) to make a projected $30 000 profit (10% of $300 000 equals $30 000).

How is this information useful?

You now have the parameters to start looking for a suitable area to buy. In other words, you need an area where unrenovated properties can be purchased for around $300 000 and renovated properties can be sold for $400 000.

This is all part of the process of establishing criteria for the type of property that is right for you. The aim is to have clear financial parameters against which to assess any property you are considering buying.

On the road to financial freedom...

Getting clear on the numbers is a great way to begin looking for renovation deals. We'll expand on this in the next chapter when we look at the 15-minute suburb search.

A critical part of developing expertise in any strategy is crunching the numbers. It is important to note that the calculations presented in this chapter are specific to a cosmetic renovation deal, although the process of number crunching a different strategy is much the same. For example, a buy–reno–subdivide–sell deal will have the following costs that you must take into account:

➤ purchase price

➤ closing costs

➤ holding costs

➤ renovation costs

➤ subdivision costs

➤ selling costs.

Take some time now and have a go at creating your own formula for the strategy you are looking to adopt for your investing. The key to doing this successfully is thoroughly researching the costs involved and creating an accurate model.

Tying it all together

By now you can probably see how everything is starting to come together. We've looked at finding your *why*, establishing your goals, calculating how much time and money you have available and how much risk you are prepared to take on, assessing your strengths and weaknesses, whether you want hands on or hands off and lump-sum or cash flow. Now we've crunched some numbers to help you understand the finances of a deal. This is all about finding a strategy and a deal that are right for *you*.

🥤 🥤 🥤

Now we're going to hear from Troy S. (We have two Troys in the book, so we'll call them Troy S and Troy H.) He's going to tell us about his deal and how he chose his strategy.

Real deal: cosmetic renovation

Hi, my name is Troy. I am 31 years old and married with a baby daughter. I run my own carpentry business and I'm also a property investor.

I enjoy my carpentry business but I don't think what I'm doing is sustainable long term. Even though I'm only 31 my back isn't holding up too well because of the work I do. I decided a while ago that I needed to start looking at other ways to earn an income. The main reason I chose property to increase my wealth is because I've always been interested in houses and as a carpenter I thought my skills would be useful. I always believed property was the quickest way to reach financial freedom.

My strategy

I chose cosmetic renovation as a strategy because I think it is a safer option when starting out, and also because renovation is something I've done before in my work and I'm quite comfortable with it. I was looking to minimise my risk as much as possible in this deal; choosing a strategy I am familiar with helped me to do this.

My deal

My first renovation deal was a little one-bedroom flat in a neat and tidy block of around 12 flats in Essendon. It was on the top level in a great location, right near a cafe strip and only 150 metres from a train station.

I found the property through developing a relationship with an agent. I had spent quite a few months researching the area and getting to know all the prominent agents in the area, and then focused my time on building relationships with the good ones. Then I received a call from one of them regarding this property, asking if I would like to have first look at it. I had been making offers on properties leading up to this so they knew I was serious, and I had also gone through exactly what I was looking for with them so when it popped up they could call me straight away.

When this property came up I could see immediately that it fit my criteria. I made an offer and secured the property, and so I got to work straight away.

> **On the road to financial freedom...**
>
> Building a very strong relationship with a real estate agent will get you at the top of their list of buyers. This will give you access to properties that have just been listed before they hit the market or before any advertising is seen by other people.

Because I like to plan ahead, I was ready to start renovation work as soon as I settled on the property. The renovation took around five weeks, which is quick. I had gained access to the unit prior to settlement, then gone in and taken all the measurements and ordered all the supplies I would need. Everything was waiting at the door when I was given the keys.

Being a one-bedroom apartment there was no outside work to be done, which is great for keeping costs and time down. All I really needed to do was make everything attractive, new and shiny, so that when people walked in they were wowed by the apartment. It was a small place so there wasn't much to do, and I decided not to do any structural work. It got a new kitchen, floorboards in the kitchen and dining room, new carpet in the bedroom, new fittings in the bathroom, it was retiled throughout, had new door handles and a glass hallway door installed, new blinds and it was painted throughout. Doing a lot of the work myself meant I could control the schedule pretty well during the renovation.

When the work was complete I gave the property back to the agent I bought it from to repay the favour and build the relationship. He worked very hard for me and found a buyer for the property who was prepared to pay the right price. I made sure I was involved in the marketing by writing the ad myself. When it is your project you will always be able to bring the most passion to the marketing. The sales campaign took about four weeks, and the settlement was 60 days.

On the road to financial freedom...

By reducing the time you take to renovate you can lower the holding costs. If you are also able to reduce the reno costs it is possible to make well in excess of 10 per cent profit on your purchase price, as Troy did.

The figures

The figures for the deal are shown in table 6.4.

Table 6.4: real deal figures

Purchase price	$182 000
Closing costs	$8 700
Time	4 months
Holding costs	$6 000
Reno costs	$8 500
Selling costs	$7 700
Sale price	$246 000
Profit	**$33 100**

Meeting the neighbours

As I was coming to the end of the project and getting ready for sale, I was noticing a concerning smell coming from the apartment next door, which was basically the smell of an illegal substance. I was worried, thinking no-one was going to buy an apartment if they turned up to the open for inspection and realised they would be living next to some extremely relaxed people. So that I didn't get offside with this neighbour, I typed a mock letter from the body corporate stating there were numerous complaints from other tenants regarding the smell coming from this person's apartment and if they did not stop it would be reported to the police. I then slid it under their door one day—funnily enough, the smell wasn't there after that. Problem solved!

Planning ahead

One of the reasons this deal worked out so well is because I prepared for the renovation before taking possession of the property. This gave me time to plan, shop around and find good deals on supplies, and also meant that I was ready to start work as soon as I was given the keys. Getting early access to the property gave me an extra eight weeks to take measurements and photos and line up the other tradies. The day I was given the keys I started work.

On the road to financial freedom...

With cosmetic renos you can really keep your costs down by shopping around and being well prepared.

Knowing the numbers

I was very comfortable with the numbers on this deal. I had such a specific idea of what I was looking for that I have passed over deals that didn't fit my criteria by just a few thousand dollars. I'd drawn up a map of the area and marked on it the sales price of every unit that had sold recently. I knew the buying costs, closing costs, knew the expected length of the project, how much the reno should cost, the selling costs and the expected selling price.

When I found this property I knew straight away that it fit my criteria. One-bedroom units were in high demand in the area, so I was confident of achieving my selling price. I just had to find one that fit my desired buy price, which this property did. My figures for this deal turned out to be very accurate; I received just a couple of grand more than I had expected when I sold, which was of course a nice bonus.

I had focused on one-bedroom units and I knew them back-to-front; I didn't worry about two-bedroom units or townhouses. I wasn't trying to break new ground or re-invent the wheel, so there was plenty of evidence available for this type of strategy. That made life a lot easier.

My wife helped me to stage the property for sale. We spent $500 at Ikea and put in a small dining table all set up, a couch, a timber frame I made up with a blow-up camp mattress for the bed, a couple of pictures, a TV unit, a mirror and towels in the bathroom. Basically the aim was to demonstrate to people how they could go about living there and how you could set up each area.

On the road to financial freedom...

When staging, it's not about putting in furniture that will last the test of time, it just needs to look great while people are inspecting the property. A bed made of empty cardboard boxes with a doona cover on it has the same visual impact as a $3000 mattress on a base (as long as nobody sits on it!).

Knowing the area and the market

Before purchasing this property I went to every open inspection in the area for units like this. I found that the target market was young professionals, because the area was within five kilometres of the CBD and close to a cafe strip. These people were looking for a nice, clean apartment that they could move straight into. They also like apartments because they are low maintenance — no gardening or mowing! I renovated the property with these people in mind. I also spent a lot of time talking to agents to get their feedback on the area and the market.

Tips for improving the presentation of a property for sale

My tips for presenting a property are:

> De-clutter everything. Simple and minimal is usually best.

> Always stage your property. A good staging job will return so much more than you outlay on the staging.

> ➤ Make everything as new and as shiny as possible. Get people saying 'wow' as soon as they walk in.

> ➤ Make the property feel homely so that potential purchasers can imagine themselves living there.

Tips for new investors

My tips for new investors are:

> ➤ Pick an area and get to know it back-to-front, so when a great deal pops up you recognise it and can act quickly.

> ➤ It's vital to build good relationships with good agents to make sure you get called first.

> ➤ Start safe and small and grow with each deal.

My current situation

I still run my own small carpentry business only two days a week. This keeps the cash flow coming in, which is important for day-to-day living and keeps the banks happy. As far as investing goes, I have now moved into property development and have our second development underway, and this takes up the rest of my time.

Although very busy, I also have the flexibility of not answering to a boss and doing things when I choose to. My family comes first and I love that I have the flexibility to make sure I am there when they need me.

Looking to the future

I am currently 31 years old and have always wanted to be financially free by 35. I'm now onto my second development deal. The main aim is to keep developing as it allows me to move away from the physical work and leverage my time a great deal more.

I have no huge desire to drive around in fancy cars or live in a mansion. My family means absolutely everything to me. Property is all about getting my time back so I can spend the absolute maximum time possible at home with my wife and baby daughter. That's what drives me to become financially free. It's all about choice. It means being able to get up every morning and spend large chunks of time with my family, and actually having the choice of whether I want to work or not.

🎁 🎁 🎁

Cosmetically renovating units can be great for investors who are just getting started. This deal was a great success for Troy because he planned ahead and was ready to start as soon as he got the keys, and he also knew his numbers and his target market very well.

Do something!

If a cosmetic reno is for you, use the methods outlined in this chapter to work out how much you could pay for a cosmetic renovation deal, given the amount of cash you have available. Or, if you have another strategy in mind, adjust the assumptions in the calculations to suit your strategy and use the appropriate numbers for your financial situation to determine the buy and sell prices for your deal.

Bonus content

To hear Troy speak about this deal in more detail, go to <www.resultsmentoring.com/book1/>.

Chapter 7

Renovations

Not all deals go according to plan. In fact some go off plan by a very long way! In this chapter we are going to hear from Katie, who will share two reno deals with us, one that was a success and one that went very wrong. There are valuable lessons in both. Inexperience often leads to mistakes, and that's what happened to Katie in her first deal.

We're also going to have a look at the 15-minute suburb search, which is a quick and easy way to find areas with good reno potential. The art of buying is the easy part but the art of profit means you must be able to sell your property for the price you expect. The 15-minute suburb search gives you the best chance to nail both.

Hands on, lump-sum cash/equity

Cash/equity requirements

- Medium amount of money required for a deposit and closing costs, depending upon property purchase price
- Medium amount of additional money required each month to fund the cosmetic reno

Borrowing capacity requirements

- Low/high amount of borrowing dependent upon the price of the property
- Medium amount of ongoing cash required to service the debt of the vacant property

Complexity/risk

- Low complexity, medium/high risk for lump-sum cash profit

Skills requirements

- Medium levels of researching, area and deal analysis and negotiation skills will be required
- Medium/high levels of project management and people skills will be required
- Medium/high handyman skills if DIY

Time requirements

- Medium time will be needed to find, analyse, negotiate and buy property
- Medium/high time will be required to execute the reno

Desired outcome

- Cash lump-sum profit or equity gain upon sale of property

Renovations

Costs: High / Medium / Low

Complexity/risk: Low / Medium / High

On the road to financial freedom ...

Most good property deals don't reach the mainstream advertising channels. You must develop relationships with real estate agents to hear about them, and to do that you must demonstrate to the agents that you are a well-informed and serious buyer.

Finding a deal: the 15-minute suburb search

Property investing is not an exact science. There are so many variables that it's impossible to accurately predict the exact profit you will make in any one deal. This suburb search is an approach to narrow your field of selection quickly and efficiently. Accuracy in the numbers will only come with extensive due diligence in the suburbs of your choice. Let's get into it.

If you are planning to increase the value of a property in a short time, you must do this in an area where buyers are willing to pay a premium for a well-presented property. It's no good buying where the average house price is $250000 and aiming to fix up and sell a property for $550000. People who can afford $550000 will be looking in other suburbs, and you will have overcapitalised on your renovation. The 15-minute suburb search is a quick and easy way to narrow down where you can buy your reno deal based on how much you can spend on a property and how much you expect to sell it for after the reno is complete.

Let's say you have:

➤ $100000 in cash and/or equity to put into an investment property

➤ the capacity to borrow another $300000

➤ chosen a cosmetic reno strategy.

As we saw in chapter 6, if $100 000 cash is available, this translates into a purchase price of around $250 000 for a reno project. And for a reno deal you should be aiming to sell the property for about 33 per cent more than you bought it for to achieve the desired profit, so:

$$\$250\,000 \times 133\% = \$332\,500$$

So you need to buy your unrenovated property for around $250 000 and be able to sell your renovated property for $332 500. The median value for a suburb where you will most likely be able to achieve this will be approximately $310 000 (which is about two-thirds of the difference between your buy and sell prices).

The 10-step process to pinpoint where you can find such properties is as follows:

1   Get a street directory map of where you live.

2   Draw a circle on your map that represents the furthest distance you are willing to travel to visit your investment property (recommended not further than 30 minutes by car).

3   List the suburb closest to you, and continue spiralling out and listing the suburbs until you hit the line you have drawn.

4   Get the latest *Australian Property Investor* magazine or some other publication that contains a median price report for each suburb by postcode.

5   Next to every suburb entry on your list, write down the median price according to the report.

6   Look for every suburb where the median price closely matches your targeted median price; in this case, $310 000.

7   The first suburb on your list where your target suburb price matches the target median price is where you begin to look for your reno deal.

8   Once you have identified your suburb, begin to research the price difference between unrenovated properties and renovated properties in that area. You can do this on <www.realestate.com.au> or <www.realestate.co.nz> and look at the different asking prices for both unrenovated and renovated properties that are up for sale. If the difference is higher than 25 per cent, keep looking in this suburb. If not, move on to the next matching suburb on your list.

9   When you have found a 25 per cent or greater differential, buy a report on all property sales in the suburb over the last 12 months. (There are various services that provide this, such as RP Data or Australian Property Monitors, for example.) Sort the report by street name.

10 Study this report and look for sales history where there is evidence of a 33 per cent differential spread in prices within the same street. When you find this it's time to get in the car and drive the street.

This will give you a great starting point to review unrenovated properties that are for sale in the streets most likely to yield the profit result you are after, in the suburb where the numbers will work with your financial circumstances.

If there are no matches, you have a number of options:

➤   If you are looking in a 30-minute radius where most postcode medians are lower, check out deals with lower buy prices and less risk.

➤   If you are looking in a 30-minute radius where postcode medians are higher, you can look further out, but be prepared to drive more.

> If you are looking in an area where postcode medians are higher, you can look to borrow more money (perhaps get a 90 per cent loan rather than an 80 per cent loan). This will allow you to buy an unrenovated property for a higher price, but it does increase your debt exposure and potentially your costs (due to lenders mortgage insurance charges on higher loan-to-valuation ratio loans).

If there is no way to make the numbers match, perhaps another strategy might be better for you at this time, or be prepared to travel.

On the road to financial freedom...

Long-service leave might be a good opportunity to undertake a renovation deal.

Reno tips

Here are some reno tips that may help you save some time and money:

> *Salvage what you can.* Don't automatically replace appliances and other items just because they are old. If something is in good working order and can be cleaned up, leave it! You can make better use of your money.

> *Avoid plumbing, electrical and structural work unless it's absolutely necessary.* Plumbing and wiring are seldom the first thing someone thinks about when they walk into a house that they might buy. Renos are all about making a good first impression so spend your money on things that will make this happen.

➤ *If you are doing the work yourself, be careful what you destroy while you're working.* You can create more work—and expense—for yourself by carelessly knocking in a wall and damaging the plumbing, or removing cupboards and accidentally taking half the wall with them.

➤ *Sometimes less is more.* An open and spacious atmosphere is more welcoming than busy and cluttered. Don't go overboard with decorating and furnishing when staging the property.

➤ *Don't forget the outside.* Your property must have 'street appeal'. Most people will simply pull up in their car and have a quick look at the place to see if it's worth a closer inspection. Your property can be a palace inside, but if you don't remove the rusty car parts, broken lawn mower and leaky wading pool from the front yard some potential buyers won't even get in the door. But if the exterior is well presented, not only will you get more people through the door, they'll already feel an attachment to the place when they get inside. This is known as 'emotional buy-in'. (It has been suggested that for each dollar you spend on the inside you'll get two dollars back, and for every dollar you spend on the outside you'll get four dollars back.)

On the road to financial freedom...

First impressions count. Focus your renovation on what potential buyers will see in the first 60 seconds of arriving at the property.

Now let's hear about Katie's deals. The first one was, well, a learning experience. The second deal went a bit more according to plan.

🏠 🏠 🏠

Real deal: a reno deal goes south

Hello. My name is Katie and I live in Sydney. I'm 30 years old, and married to Beau. Our first reno deal was, shall we say, not a great success, but we've persevered and learned from our mistakes and we've done much better with our second deal. Hopefully you'll be able to see some of the mistakes we made and not repeat them!

We're relatively new to real estate. Prior to getting married, Beau had owned and sold two negative cash flow townhouses on the Sunshine Coast. He'd done quite well with these, and this encouraged us to look into property further. Our goal is eventually for both of us to be able to leave work, and we thought property might be the way to do it. This deal was our first together.

How to lose $100 000

Our first cosmetic renovation was a two-bedroom house in the Blue Mountains, NSW. We decided on renovation because we wanted to build our capital in a short period of time and we felt that renovating would be a good place to begin.

We decided that I would quit my job as a speech pathologist and work five days a week on the renovation, and Beau would continue working as a project manager for an IT company to support us financially. After making this decision, we began scouring internet sites for a potential suburb that could support this strategy. We were looking for a suburb that had a large difference between the cheaper and more expensive properties (thus a significant range in prices) and properties that we could afford. We thought that this would give us the opportunity to buy at the lower end and sell at the higher end of the market.

After six months of looking, we were quite frustrated about not finding a potential project. It was around this time that we came across the suburb of Blackheath, in the Blue Mountains.

This suburb appeared to offer a glimmer of hope. There was a large price difference between the cheaper properties and the more expensive properties and it seemed to us that people were willing to pay more for a renovated property. However, at this early stage and having just started investigating the area, we didn't fully understand why that price gap existed (ominous warning number one that I missed). We began inspecting properties every weekend. It was quite a drive, one and a half hours from our home, and so it required planning and some sacrifices.

After finding no promising properties, I had another look at all the properties that were available for sale. I decided to go through one that was advertised on <www.realestate.com.au> as having been recently painted and as being in a neat and tidy condition with newish carpets. I didn't really think it would fit our criteria, but having nothing else to look at I decided I might as well check it out.

A renovator's delight!

I met the agent at the property and quickly realised that the house was in a worse state than I was anticipating. (Ominous warning number two that I missed.) It was a two-bedroom house that had been modified from its original floor plan. The block was small (385 square metres) and narrow and there was no off-street parking. The house also had no street appeal and the gardens were a hodgepodge of weeds and very old plants. Some of the property description was correct though. The property had recently been painted … a mix of pink, cream, blue, green, white and brown; and the carpet was fairly new, but the cheap kind that even landlords no longer put in their properties! The layout was not functional and the backyard was overgrown. There was also a makeshift sunroom. This house was in dire need of TLC. While many would see a renovation on this property as time consuming and costly, I saw 'potential potential, potential'.

Ideally, the plan for this property was to do a straightforward, strictly cosmetic renovation that would cost a maximum of 10 per cent of the purchase price ($22 500) and would take no longer than six months. We felt if we stuck to this reno budget this project would return us a neat profit of about $22 000 (about 10 per cent of the purchase price).

The property was advertised for $230 000. We offered $220 000 and the vendors counter-offered with $225 000, which we agreed on. If we had done more research, we would have learned that this property had already been on the market with three different agents and had been on the market with the current agent for at least two months. (Ominous warning number three that I missed.) So while we thought $225 000 was a reasonable price, there were in fact good reasons why no one else had wanted to purchase this house.

The downward spiral...

Buoyed by our purchase, we wasted no time in getting started. First to come off were the fake wooden panels, plaster, carpet and lino that were lining the inside of the house. The removal of the internal linings revealed quite a surprise: underneath were all of the original features of the house: the timber walls, Baltic pine floors and timber ceilings. We had mixed feelings about this finding though as we didn't know how much extra work was involved in preparing and painting these surfaces. Most of the paintwork was intact; however, some boards were chipped, some were missing or substituted with mismatched timber, and there were some large gaps in the boards as a result of natural shrinkage over time. Removal of the linings also revealed large gaping holes that remained where the original front and side windows and the front door had been. This meant we would have to either reconfigure/replace the original timber boards to cover the holes or relocate the existing windows and doors to their original locations. (Ominous warning number four that I missed.) Both these options were going to be much more costly that what we had budgeted.

With the benefit of hindsight, I can now say that at the time of purchasing we really didn't recognise this house for what it was: an original 100-year-old timber miner's cottage. This was partly due to not having been through many of these types of houses and partly due to the house having undergone various redesigns by various owners since its construction in the early 1900s.

A change in plans

Faced with this dilemma, a more experienced renovator may have reclad, prettied up and sold the house very quickly. We, however, were inexperienced and became emotionally involved as we saw amazing potential in this character home. We wanted to return the house to its former glory, so we decided to re-think our plan. Rather than do a quick-turn cosmetic renovation, we decided to completely renovate this property back to its original state with some additional structural improvements. We felt that this style of renovation, while different from our original plans, would allow us to present a property that would appeal to a more cashed-up target market: the weekender market. We also figured that by appealing to the higher end of the market, people would pay more and so our costs would be covered and our profit margin for this deal would increase. We set about deciding on and implementing a new design.

It seemed like a good idea at the time ... Later we would see this as the first poorly researched decision that would lead to budget blowouts.

Blue Mountains Council were very happy with our plans as our renovation would increase the appeal of the property and also the street, which had a heritage overlay. What they were less thrilled about was our attempt to get the addition of a carport approved with our development application. Our block, being one of the earliest in the area, was 385 square metres and quite narrow. We wanted off-street undercover parking but we only had one option for the location of the carport and that was to the right side of the house. Unfortunately for us, there was a huge conifer in the way. Initially, the council wouldn't allow us to remove it. Finally they agreed it could be removed, but the condition was that the carport would have to be placed behind the house. Placing the carport at the rear of the block was not appealing as the block fell away at the back and it was a good 20 metres from the front to the rear boundary. If we put a carport down the back, future owners would need to reverse out of the carport then another 15 metres down a narrow driveway. We decided this would not be practical or reasonable and so abandoned our plans of getting undercover, off-street parking. We were really unhappy with this outcome but realised we were wasting time and money on holding costs trying to convince the council to change their mind.

On the road to financial freedom ...

If a deal starts to go seriously wrong, sometimes it's better to cut your losses early and get out. If you decide to continue you must be confident that this will produce the best outcome for you – don't keep going just because you are stubborn or are hoping for the best. As always, do your sums and base your decision on the numbers.

We went ahead with the rest of our structural plans. The best quote we received from a builder was $28000 for this work. While this was more than we had anticipated, we agreed on the price. (Ominous warning ... I've lost count now. You get the idea. We should have seen it coming.)

There was still lots of work required inside and outside the house that wasn't included in the builder's quote. Some of the jobs included replacement and reconfiguration of the kitchen, stripping the bathroom and re-lining the walls and re-tiling, replacing seven windows, putting in a new wall, installing built-ins and doors, fitting out the entire house with new architraves, skirtings and door frames, paving and landscaping, staining the deck, painting internally and externally ... the list just went on and on. To save money, we decided to do as much of the work ourselves as possible. This period in the renovation was actually very enjoyable and rewarding. Our demolition efforts and removal of rubbish and overgrown trees resulted in visual improvements and we felt like we were making good progress. The non-work periods were fun, too, as we spent time with family, enjoyed 'camping' in the house, ordering takeaway pizza and watching DVDs on the laptop.

Help!

After about eight months the project became more and more difficult. We grew weary of working long hours, making slow progress, nursing aches and pains and still seeing a mountain of work ahead. To speed things up we decided to increase our hours, so I began working seven days on the project and Beau joined me on weekends in addition to working his full-time job. This did improve our progress but it drained us even more, physically and emotionally. We were beginning to lose sight of our goals and could not visualise the renovation ever being completed.

We had to make changes. We decided to get organised and arrange for tradespeople to do more of the work. I focused more on project management, and I started to calculate our costs and work out how much money we had left. While doing the figures I found that our costs had already far exceeded what we had planned on spending when we first purchased — and we were months off completion. This was a gut-wrenching realisation.

Our response to this was that we finally took action. We clamped down on spending and questioned every cost.

We worked very hard to get the project finished, and our management skills improved out of sight. The renovation was rocketing along and our tradespeople were invaluable, but our costs were mounting and it wasn't long before we hit another painful hurdle. We were fast running out of money and could no longer finance the completion of the project ourselves. We scrambled for a solution, and decided to refinance our loan. This kept us going for a while but costs continued to mount and we eventually required another cash injection in the form of a personal loan. This was a horrible option and the interest rate was horrendous, but we were desperate!

On the road to financial freedom...

If your people skills are better than your handyman skills, pay others to do the work.

Selling at a bad time

The financial crisis unfolding in the US had reached Australia's shores and had sent the stock market into a tailspin. Soon enough, Australia's real estate market was also feeling the combined effects of consumer trepidation and evaporation of money from the financial markets. Our timing for the sale of our property could not have been worse. Our auction campaign was planned to begin in June 2008 and our house was due to be sold in the first week of July. What made this situation worse still was that our target market, the cashed-up Sydney buyers looking to spend their surplus funds on a weekender, were the ones being hardest hit, especially in the sharemarket.

Marketing and staging the property

We took the sales and marketing campaign for the sale of our property very seriously. Too often we had seen property owners put enormous amounts of effort into the renovation or construction of a property, only to then fail to create a customised campaign that actually attracted their intended buyer. We wanted to do things differently, and we decided to furnish the house for the sale process. Some of the rooms were smallish so we wanted to demonstrate to buyers how the furniture could be arranged and what might fit in each room. As we were targeting the weekender market, we also wanted to give the house a relaxed, warm feel, while simultaneously demonstrating to buyers that this house provided an escape from the frantic pace of Sydney. To achieve this we planned to light the fire, put on some soothing background music, turn down the lighting, decorate with some fresh flowers and light our coffee-scented candles so the aroma would waft throughout the house.

Unfortunately, the team behind the sales people in the real estate office weren't on the ball and the marketing material for our property was incorrect on four separate occasions, with an incorrect title, price or photo. Unfortunately, all these errors were made on printed material already available to the public and they could not be easily fixed. The repeated errors became very irritating as we had paid for these marketing extras. This experience did demonstrate to us that despite our best efforts there are always things that will be out of your control.

Our first open house was a resounding success — in terms of buyer response. We had 17 couples through the property. The following three opens also attracted good numbers of buyers. Our agent told us that our sales and marketing campaign had yielded the best buyer enquiry level ever and it was likely the best campaign his agency had ever run. We were chuffed! But what was more important was what people thought, and that wasn't such good news. Our agent relayed the buyer feedback that he had collected during each inspection. Many buyers liked the character of the property, the renovation and the presentation, but they needed a larger block and off-street, undercover parking. Some also said they would have liked a third bedroom and an extra living space and would have preferred the house be located in a completely different area of town!

On the road to financial freedom...

Before you get started on a reno, do some research into what your buyers want. Don't assume that just making the house prettier will attract a buyer.

It was disappointing that we could not do anything to accommodate the buyers' needs. Over the course of our marketing campaign it became increasingly obvious that our property did not suit our target buyers and we had selected a difficult market with very specific tastes. While we had anticipated buyers would want an undercover car space for their BMWs and Porsches, we had not anticipated that people would like more land. We made the mistake of thinking that more land would mean more maintenance, and people wouldn't want that in a weekender. We had been caught out thinking from our own perspective of maintaining the property, rather than from the perspective that these buyers would be paying gardeners to do this. Another thing we didn't realise was that this market had expensive tastes in fixtures and fittings, and while we had put some good-quality finishes in the property, it was still not up to scratch for these buyers. Lastly, these buyers were not in a hurry to purchase a weekender as it would be a second home, and price was less important than finding a property that fit all their criteria. All these issues raised by buyers now demonstrated to us why properties in Blackheath ranged so much in price. It also helped us to understand that we really had not done enough research on the suburb, had not gone through enough comparable properties listed for sale, had not studied our target buyer market, and had not realised that the market we were trying to appeal to represented a very small, niche group of people.

So to sum it up, we had chosen a difficult buyer market of which we had little understanding, whose numbers were steadily dwindling (thanks to the GFC) and our product did not even come close to meeting their needs. Awesome!

On the road to financial freedom...

Mistakes are just learning experiences. There are valuable lessons in them. Figure out where you went wrong, and then pick yourself up and keep going. Persistence will have you win in the end.

Well, at least we got rid of it...

The day of the execution...um, auction...was one of the most anxious we'd ever experienced. Only two parties had registered to bid. We were advised by our agent that one was unrealistic and wanted to buy the property for $100 000 less than we were willing to sell it for. Our uneasiness mounted. Only one serious bidder does not make for a good auction. The bidding started very low. It slowly built and then halted, and only one bidder remained. A vendor bid was used and this encouraged one more bid. Without another competing party, the bids naturally dried up. Beau and I had already discussed our reserve price, but it was still $35 000 higher than the current bid. The agent came to speak with us but we weren't ready to move on that price; we were in shock. So our property was passed in and the auction was wound up. Our agent gingerly approached us to see if we were interested in negotiating with the highest bidder. We were, and so he got started. He was successful in getting the buyer to increase their offer by another $10 000, but that was it. This took the offer to $350 000. He left us so we could think it over. We were in great despair.

Working out whether to accept this offer was one of the most difficult decisions we've ever had to make. On the one hand, we knew we were going to make a loss: exactly how much we weren't sure but we were trying to cap it. On the other hand we also knew that the hype and suspense that we had created in our marketing campaign would vanish after the auction, and there would be a high possibility that we would not receive another offer of more than $350 000. Not to mention the holding costs were significant and with every day that the property remained on the market our losses would further increase. When the decision was made, it was devastating. We decided to accept the offer of $350 000.

In total, we lost close to $100 000 on this project and the reno took 16 months to complete. The costs would have been even higher if we hadn't been fortunate enough to have our fathers doing some of the work, saving us at least $10 000. (Here's a tip: families are a great source of cheap labour. But make sure you employ the right family member!) How we could spend $100 000 without actually noticing at the time is difficult to understand. It's very disheartening to know that you would have more money in your pocket if you had just spent your time going to the beach instead.

As they say, though, it is water under the bridge and we have dealt with it and accepted it. Today we are comfortable telling people if they ask about previous projects. We have evaluated the experience and really learned so much from it. More importantly, we have since applied our learning to subsequent projects and now we are happy to help others to learn from it too. Experiences like this leave a lasting impression!

The figures

Our figures for the deal are as shown in table 7.1.

Table 7.1: real deal figures

	Ideal figures	Actual figures
Purchase price	$225 000	$225 000
Closing costs	$11 000	$14 000
Time	6 months	18 months
Holding costs	$9 500	Lots! ($40 000+)
Reno costs	$22 500	$155 000
Selling costs	$10 000	$15 000
Sale price	$300 000	$350 000
Profit	**$22 000**	**I wish**

Getting the sales price we were after may at least seem like a positive, but it wasn't. In our dreams we wanted $350 000 just for the cosmetic renovation; after our change of plans we hoped for a much higher price. So we basically spent a lot more time and money and didn't increase our sales price at all. Let's move on quickly...

On the road to financial freedom...

Property investing is never without risk and few successful investors have never made a loss at some point. Treat a loss as a lesson that you can learn from to improve your skills so that you don't make the same mistakes again.

Luckily for us, we had no choice but to continue our future in property renovation. We had purchased and had already been living in our next renovation project for over 12 months. So, within two months of selling the property in Blackheath, we had moved out of the next project and begun renovating our next property in Blacktown. This time things were going to be different.

Real deal: reno success

After our first reno debacle, we were determined to find a property closer to home for our next deal.

In August 2007, while doing a property search of suburbs in the west of Sydney, I found a property on <www.realestate.com.au> that caught my interest. It stood out because it appeared to be staggeringly cheap, relative to all other houses in the suburb. The house was advertised as a three-bedroom, one-bathroom vinyl-clad home on just over 600 square metres of land in Blacktown. It was advertised for $200000. After 30 minutes of internet research, we could see this was potentially a super deal for us.

First thing the following day I called the sales agent managing the property. I wasn't the only one and later found out that the agent had been bombarded with calls from buyers also interested. I was told that the property needed a lot of work and there were easements on it. I was also told that it was not in liveable condition (it turns out that was putting it very politely!) and that it couldn't be rented out in its current state, but I wasn't dissuaded.

Researching

In the days leading up to the auction we did lots of research. At home, we researched the prices of all properties that were for sale or had been sold in the area in the last 12 months. As we did not have the opportunity to get quotes for repairs on the property, we really wanted to understand the risks associated with this purchase as best we could. All of our research revealed that the risks in purchasing this property were quite low and we couldn't find any data or information that indicated otherwise. To support our internet research, we visited the area. We inspected the outside of the house, observed the quality of the surrounding homes, spoke to agents and researched local amenities. During this time we learned that the property had been on the market for a couple weeks and it had been listed for $240 000 before being dropped to $200 000 the same day I saw the advertisement.

As the number of visitors to the property web page grew, we understood that we would have to act fast if we were going to secure this property. We crunched theoretical renovation numbers (given we hadn't seen inside the property), checked with our mortgage broker that we could get the finance and decided that we were going to do our best to buy it. We would pay the $200 000 they were asking for the property. We also made what many would describe as an insane decision. We decided we would move into the property! This decision was made because we could not afford to pay two mortgages in addition to our existing rent.

Another renovator's delight! Are we crazy?

Saturday couldn't come soon enough. We arrived to inspect the property with about 40 other buyers. Upon entering the property it was clear this house wouldn't appeal to a lot of people and we were going to have do some urgent remedial work if we were going to live there. It smelt of urine and was a mess. The carpet in the lounge and dining was originally cream — now it was black. Doors were missing; you could see daylight between the gaps in the mismatched cornice; there were holes in the floorboards and walls; in the wet areas there were mismatched tiles and fixtures; and it seemed the owners had begun demolishing the original kitchen and installing two new laundries, but had abandoned the idea. Evidence of their previous handy work were three incomplete laundries and two incomplete kitchens. Weird! The tiles, fan and lino of the original kitchen remained in situ, and the 'new' kitchen, which was secondhand, was barely functional and had been roughly assembled to fit in the existing space. There was no oven, and the stove and rangehood had never been wired in. If you look up 'fixer-upper' in the dictionary there's a picture of this place.

The roof in the kitchen was covered in water stains and clearly leaked. While this would not be good for us as residents, it was a skillion roof so we knew it wouldn't cost a lot to have this replaced. What was really gross was that the walls in the house were covered with a visible layer of grime and in some rooms there were unrecognisable coloured stains running down the walls. The house appeared not to have been cleaned in years.

Did this explain the low asking price? Despite being a visual disgrace, I didn't think so as most of the work that was required appeared to be cosmetic. The actual structure and floor plan was reasonable and all the bedrooms were large, much larger than average for the area. The external vinyl cladding was in great condition, as were half of the windows. What was potentially a problem and which would have affected the asking price was that there was no driveway to the property, and being situated at the bottom of a cul-de-sac there was on-street parking for only one car.

What could complicate and perhaps even hinder the approval of a driveway and carport was that there was a drainage easement that ran the length of the left boundary and also the rear fence and had a width of almost three metres. While we knew of other people who had received council approval to install driveways and carports over drainage easements, we realised we may not be so lucky and so there was still a level of risk in the project. The absence of a driveway and the existence of the easement was publicised by the agent, who was also very vocal in her opinion that council would not allow a driveway to be constructed. This, in addition to the presentation of the property, clearly put off many buyers. Good news for us!

After the inspection I called the agent. We were told that another buyer had made an offer. I immediately offered $203 000. The offer was the highest and was accepted. I received another call shortly after and we were told the other buyer had increased their offer. We increased ours to $210 000. The agent said she'd take it to the owner but as it was late we were told that the vendor would think it over and we would be called in the morning. After some hassles and negotiating our offer was accepted.

After settlement of the property I ordered a skip and got to work. The thought of moving into the house was bad enough, but there was no way we were going to live there with the black carpet still present. I ripped it all up. Unsurprisingly, the underlay was also filthy and it went too. Thankfully, that solved the problem of the smell of urine. I then cleaned every surface as much as I could. The amount of grime that came off the walls was alarming but after three days of cleaning it was ready for us to move in. The day we began moving things in to the property, the reality of our situation suddenly became very apparent. We looked at each other and wondered what on earth we were doing there.

Adding a bedroom and ensuite

We'd done some planning but still needed to make some final decisions about what exactly we wanted to do. We realised there was potential to create a smaller fourth bedroom by moving a wall and reducing the size of the extra large living space.

Looking at other properties that were on the market, there were very few four-bedroom houses available. Discussions with agents also revealed that four-bedroom houses were in high demand. However, we didn't know whether doing this would increase the value of the house enough to justify the cost of doing it. This time we also wanted to make the decision based on real numbers, not estimates, opinion or emotion. To answer this we had to work out the price difference between three- and four-bedroom homes. We paid for a report that listed all the properties that had sold in Blacktown over the last 12 months. As Blacktown is a very large suburb and there are over 600 properties sold every year, there was a lot of data to look at. I found a big difference between the three- and four-bedroom homes and so the decision to convert our property into a four-bedroom house became an easy one.

We also had another opportunity to modify the floor plan for the better. As there was unused plumbing in the original laundry, it was a decent size and it already had a toilet attached to it, we knew it would be straightforward to convert it into an ensuite. We worked out the price of converting the laundry into an ensuite and then compared the sales prices of four-bedroom, one-bathroom houses with four-bedroom, two-bathroom houses. The results clearly indicated that it would be more profitable for us to create the ensuite. An easy decision yet again!

Having made these decisions we were in a position to get a better understanding of our target market. Discussions with agents revealed that first or second home buyers would be most likely to purchase properties with floor plans like ours if the property could remain affordable. We crunched numbers on the renovation, keeping in mind the minimum sales price we were anticipating for the property was $350000 and we were expecting a profit of at least $30000. While there was a bit of room for spending on the renovation, we didn't want to commit to spend all the renovation budget because we wanted to allow a margin for unplanned costs.

On the road to financial freedom...

Buyers at the higher end of the market are looking for features and comfort; buyers at the lower end of the market are looking for value and affordability.

The renovations

We decided to do the following work in our renovation:

➤ cut down trees at front of house and put in a new fence

➤ add new carport and driveway (we'd received council approval!)

➤ put in new laminate kitchen

➤ add new ensuite

➤ renovate existing bathroom (put in new bath, new toilet, new vanity and new shower screen, re-tile shower)

➤ move a wall to create new bedroom

➤ re-line and tile new laundry

➤ paint internal

➤ paint roof

➤ landscape

➤ polish floorboards

➤ put in new carpet

➤ add new doors, skirtings, architraves.

We applied what we had learned from our first deal. We chose to do much less hands-on work ourselves and we also decided to give our dads a break and pay for tradespeople to do the hard work. When we began the renovation we anticipated that the whole project (including the sales process) would take us six months. This time frame blew out to 10 months due to my underestimating how long some jobs would take and the Christmas break bringing tradespeople and suppliers to a halt. However, we were very happy with the final result! The finished house is shown in figure 7.1.

Figure 7.1: completed renovation

Marketing and staging the property

We decided to market the house exactly as we had for our property in Blackheath. We staged the property. We furnished three out of four bedrooms, and the lounge and dining rooms. We also hung paintings, and used vases, candles and books. We wrote the copy and organised for professional photographs. Similarly to Blackheath, we also put a lot of consideration into our selection of an agent. While inspecting properties across the Blacktown area, we had come to know the agents quite well. We learned a lot by listening to what they told other buyers, by asking them direct and pointed questions and by making note of whether they followed us up as potential buyers.

We interviewed three real estate agents, and they gave us vastly different sales prices. The agent we selected estimated we would sell the house for $375 000, which was the highest estimate, but that's not why we chose him. The truth was that our research and sales data indicated that his estimate was spot on.

As the market was strong and our property would be in demand, he felt that we should sell the house without a price tag, instead using 'Express Sale'. We were unsure about this but he recalled numerous sales where he had used this method with great success and he fully explained how he negotiated these types of sales. His argument was convincing and we were impressed by his insight into the sales process and by his negotiation methods.

On the road to financial freedom...

A good real estate agent can make a big difference to your deal, so make sure you interview at least three agents and choose the one with the best track record for selling properties like yours.

Sold in 10 days!

Our first open for inspection attracted a lot of buyers. We received two offers. One was for $340 000 and the other was from a first home buyer for $350 000. We didn't accept them. The second open home attracted more buyers and another offer of $360 000. The couple that offered $350 000 the previous weekend also took their parents through. They increased their offer to $370 000. We didn't accept this but told the agent that we would accept $375 000. He got the buyers up to $372 500. Knowing that this wasn't far off what we were hoping for, we said we would accept the offer only if he felt the buyers wouldn't pay $375 000. We didn't want to lose them. He said he wasn't sure but he'd see how the sales discussions progressed. Fifteen minutes later we received a call from the agent saying that he had got the buyers up to $375 000 and they were signing the contract. We were ecstatic. We'd sold the house in 10 days!

Our experience really reinforced to us the importance of being area experts and interviewing a number of agents to sell a property. It would have been a mistake to believe that all agents know the market and what a property is worth. If we'd had less idea of our property's worth and we hadn't picked the right agent, we could have sold our property for up to $35000 less than the market was willing to pay. Our research had really paid off.

The figures

The figures for this deal are shown in table 7.2.

Table 7.2: real deal figures

	Planned figures	Actual figures
Purchase price	$210000	$210000
Closing costs	$11000	$10500
Time	8 months	10 months
Holding costs	$12000	$14500
Reno costs	$40000	$65400
Selling costs	$14000	$11600
Sale price	$320000	$375000
Profit	**$33000**	**$63000**

I much prefer these figures to those of our first deal!

Becoming an area expert

By the end of this deal, I had become what I consider an area expert in this suburb. I felt I could walk into any property for sale in Blacktown and accurately estimate the price it would sell for within $5000, even if the property didn't have any price indication at all in the sales material. I knew the market, I knew the properties and I knew who the buyers were. This gave me a great deal of confidence throughout the sale and negotiation process. As we do more deals and invest in different locations, I'll focus on becoming an area expert in more places and this will give me a big advantage in my investing. I'll know what is a reasonable price to pay for a property, and what I can expect to sell it for. It will also allow me to accurately create a budget for a project and work out in advance if a deal will be profitable. And I'll be able to keep the real estate agents honest!

On the road to financial freedom...

You must be knowledgeable about the area you are buying in, otherwise you won't know how much you should pay for a property or how much you can expect to sell it for. See if you can predict sales prices to within $5000.

Tips for staging a property

These are my tips for staging a property:

> For property inspections ensure all the blinds are open and the lights are on in darker rooms.

> Furnish at least the lounge, dining and main bedroom. Try also to use bedspreads, cushions and blinds/curtains that are of a colour and style that is in fashion in popular home stores.

> Ensure the lawn and gardens are immaculate and appear low in maintenance.

Tips for new investors

My tips for new investors are:

➤ Think about the strategy you want to try and then work out how much time you are realistically able to dedicate to it. Renovation is very hands on and when starting out you need time to learn how to project manage the deal and what your roles should be.

➤ Take action on every potential deal or opportunity, even if it takes you out of your comfort zone. You never know what the outcome could be.

➤ Become an area expert before buying a property.

➤ Interview agents at every opportunity. Choosing the right agent could make or break your deal.

My current situation

We want to do more property deals! I am now working part time while I look for deals. We are saving money to put towards our investments, and we are restricting our spending on rent, clothes, cars and so on. We have to ensure though that our budget still allows us to have an active social and sporting lifestyle and enjoy occasional holidays and weekends away. We still want to have fun!

Looking to the future

We want to become financially independent. We'd love not to have to worry about money and instead indulge our passions of travel and great food and wine, and our love of sports and trying new and exciting experiences. Another reason is to allow us to be in a position to support family and friends and others in need. We have recently set the goal to be financially free in 2015.

We are still looking for renovation projects. We are now also focusing on increasing our knowledge in the area of development.

🏠 🏠 🏠

Katie has shown the value of perseverance. After her first deal she could have easily decided that it's too hard and given up, but then she would have missed out on the great profit in her next deal. If things get tough, remember that there are always better times ahead.

Do something!

Do a 15-minute suburb search assuming the following:

- you have $100 000 in cash to put into an investment property

- you have the capacity to borrow another $300 000

- your chosen strategy is a cosmetic reno.

Now find a suburb! Everything you need to do this is written in the last few chapters. Have a go and test yourself.

Bonus content

To hear Katie speak about her deal in more detail, go to <www.resultsmentoring.com/book1/>.

Part III

Subdivisions plus

Chapter 8

Subdivisions

Subdivision is dividing a block of land into smaller parcels. From an investing point of view, the aim is to buy a property at a certain price, divide it into a number of smaller properties, and then sell these in total for more than was paid for the original property (plus costs). It's not a very complicated concept!

Let's say you have a 1500-square-metre block and can divide it into three lots of 500 square metres each. Each 500-square-metre lot is likely to be worth more than one-third of the value of the original lot. This happens because there are more buyers who can afford a smaller block with a nice house on it than a bigger block with a nice house. More buyers means more competition, which pushes up prices. This is where the profit comes from in subdivisions. And many buyers are willing to sacrifice land size in order to live closer to the CBD.

Hands on, lump-sum cash/equity

Subdivision 1 into 2

Cash/equity requirements

- Low/medium amount of money required for a deposit and closing costs, depending upon property purchase price
- Low/medium amount of additional money required to fund the simple subdivision

Borrowing capacity requirements

- Medium amount of borrowing dependent upon the size and price of a property big enough to subdivide
- Low/medium amount of money required each month to service the shortfall between rent and loan repayments

Complexity/risk

- Low/medium complexity, medium risk for lump-sum cash profit

Skills requirements

- Medium levels of researching, area and deal analysis and negotiation skills will be required
- Medium levels of project management and people skills will be required
- High levels of patience (for dealing with local authorities)

Time requirements

- Low/medium time will be needed to find, analyse, negotiate and buy property
- Low time required to execute a simple subdivision, as most day-to-day tasks are outsourced

Desired outcome

- Cash lump-sum profit upon sale of property

> **On the road to financial freedom...**
>
> For a subdivision, the parts are greater than the sum.

Subdivision is a hands-on strategy, but you don't need to be good with a hammer and nails. Time requirements are low and you can do most of the work behind a desk, though the length of a project can be long because planning authorities such as local councils can be prone to delays.

Unfortunately it's not always obvious whether a property can be subdivided. Just because you have a large block doesn't mean the council or applicable planning authority will allow a subdivision. For example, the property might be zoned 'low density' or be covered by an 'environmental' overlay that will stop you from removing trees or be subject to any other number of restrictions in the local planning scheme. Every area has slight differences in the local planning scheme so research into these restrictions is critical.

> **On the road to financial freedom...**
>
> Check zoning and planning restrictions before buying a property that you plan to subdivide. Make sure that subdivision is permissible and clarify the conditions that need to be satisfied in order to be able to split up and sell the properties.

Subdivision due diligence

You must carefully research your ability to subdivide before you commit to buying the property. If you find out after you have purchased it that your 1000-square-metre block can't be subdivided because of zoning restrictions, you've just bought yourself a big problem.

Let's have a look at some of the steps you can take to ensure your subdivision goes smoothly:

➤ Have a land surveyor give you an opinion on whether they believe the land can be subdivided. Use a local surveyor who is familiar with the local planning scheme.

➤ Have a proposed plan of the subdivision drawn up by a surveyor and checked by the council or planning authority. Note that they won't give you an official approval until you own the property and have gone through the full permit approval process. Approach your conversation from the perspective of 'tell me why this won't work'. Legally councils cannot say *yes* to anything without going through the full process, but they are quite free to say *no, this won't work*.

➤ Find out if there are any restrictions on the property, such as covenants (restrictions on how the land may be used), easements (for example, a protected sewer pipe) or overlays (such as heritage protection, flooding or environmental restrictions).

➤ If it looks like major work will be required—for example, redirecting underground pipes—consult an engineer to find out what is involved and what it may cost.

🏠 🏠 🏠

Now we are going to hear from Shilpa. Look out for how she describes in detail her ideal property. The reason you will want to describe in detail the property you are looking for is so that you can find the needle in the haystack.

Once you have determined your *why* and have clarity around your finances and borrowing capacity, are clear on your strengths and weaknesses, know a bit about the economic environment you are investing in and have chosen your strategy, your job is to determine the ideal property relative to your strategy and personal circumstances. This helps you to buy with confidence the property that you know will yield the profit that you are after. For example, if you decided you wanted to do a reno and subdivision project you'd be looking for a property on a block large enough to subdivide with a structurally sound house near the front and to one side so that a driveway can go up the side to a second block. It would also have to be at a price you could afford and still do the renovation.

Real deal: buy one, get one free (almost)

Hello. My name is Shilpa. I was trained as a doctor in India, and I was in practice for a few years before we moved to Australia in 2004. I now live in Sydney working as a consultant. I also have an online software business and work as a lecturer.

When we came to Australia we had very little money. My husband Atul got a job in IT, and I got a part-time job lecturing and also started my own business. We had a baby boy, who is now four years old. (He keeps me on my toes!) I currently work two days a week in my business and lecture for only a couple of hours a week. Before I started investing in property, this earned me around $20 000 a year in total.

In 2004 my husband and I were learning about financial freedom. We were reading books and attending seminars. We were good savers and had put away a fair bit in a few years, but we soon realised that even if we continued saving in this way we would not achieve financial freedom. We needed to do something different. Having read many wealth creation books by different authors and attended seminars, we realised that property would be a good vehicle to help us reach our financial goals. That's when Atul found a property mentoring program. Originally the plan was for him to join the program and I would help, but because he was working more hours than I was it made more sense for me to enrol in the program. This was the beginning of our real estate investing.

I had no experience whatsoever in property, and to be frank I don't think I was interested in property when I started. To me it was just another option for making money, just like shares or running a business. But after I got into it and started crunching numbers and meeting people, I really started to enjoy it.

Our goal is to generate a passive income from our investments and be financially free. This will give me the ability and means to be able to live my dream with my family and be in a position to extend myself for others who are in need.

An unexpected find

I calculated the figures on a number of different strategies in my target area. The numbers worked best for a subdivision project. While doing this research, I discovered a property on the internet. It already had two houses on one title and so was perfect for a subdivision. It is on a 638-square-metre block and situated about 30 kilometres from the Sydney CBD. Our initial figures on this property showed a profit margin that we were happy with.

The front house is a two-bedroom fibro. It is around 50 years old and was rented till recently for $300 per week. The rear house is a two-bedroom brick. It is 18 years old and was rented till recently for $350 per week. Both houses were in fair condition. The front house has a recently renovated bathroom.

The property had been on the market for around six months, and was originally listed for $600 000. We first saw the property in October 2008 and put in a verbal offer for $470 000, which was rejected by the vendor. We put in this offer because I knew the area very well and I knew what houses were selling for. We were also concerned about the house at the back of the property; the vendor didn't seem to have the legal paperwork required for the house. I made my own enquiries with the council, and it turned out that the vendor hadn't met many of the regulations when building the second house. So we basically ignored the second house when making our offer, because I was concerned that the council would tell us to knock it down. Our offer was made up of $450000 for the front house and $20000 for the back house. The vendor was very upset at this! She didn't seem to know about these problems or realise the paperwork she needed to sell the house.

The house at the back had another problem: there was termite damage. This had caused an earlier offer on the property to fall through. We knew a carpenter who came to look at the property for us. He told us that the termites had not caused any structural damage and there were no termites there now. We also had a pest inspection done which confirmed this, so we proceeded with the deal. This might have actually helped us secure the deal as it probably turned off other buyers.

A done deal

We kept looking for other deals while keeping an eye on this one. We then made a conditional offer of $495000 two days before Christmas. The price was acceptable to the vendor but the conditions were not. After a month and a half of negotiations, we signed an unconditional offer of $485000.

On the road to financial freedom ...

Traditionally property prices fall just before Christmas because vendors 'want it sold' so that they can go into the new year with a fresh perspective.

The plan for the property was:

➤ Complete a detailed survey and engineering plans prior to settlement.

➤ Rent out both properties ASAP (they would be positively geared in the current market) by asking the vendor to allow us to put the houses on the rental market and permit an open house inspection prior to settlement.

➤ Apply for subdivision to the council and other authorities.

➤ Wait for council approval, while ensuring that the properties have minimal vacancies and hence no holding costs.

➤ If approved, carry out the necessary construction work (if possible with tenants still in). There was a possibility that the subdivision would not be approved.

➤ Choose between selling both (our preferred option) and selling one or none.

We chose subdivision because it was a strategy that I could pursue without compromising my lifestyle as a full-time mother as well as a part-time businesswoman. The effort and time I put in were on research and calculating the figures, which could be done from home and on my computer. The legwork was possible with my toddler in the backseat as I drove around my target area.

The subdivision process required no work on site from me but I needed to be in touch with my team and manage them. Fortunately the deal had enough profit to be able to fund a surveyor, builder and project manager to look after the day-to-day nitty-gritties, which was not my speciality. This was all completely new to me and overwhelming at times, but the strategy worked well with my situation.

Figure 8.1 shows some pictures of the property.

The figures

The figures for the deal are shown in table 8.1 (on page 162).

Holding costs of $0 was a big benefit of this deal. Having the property positively geared from day one meant that we started earning around $100 per week as soon as we settled.

Even though we were planning to subdivide, we could still have tenants, so the extra few months to complete the project were not a problem; as it was positively geared, holding the property for longer didn't really matter.

Figure 8.1: the property

Above: front house
Right: driveway to back house

The subdivision costs are high because there were regulations that the property didn't comply with, so we had to fix these problems. We also had to build a new driveway and have car spaces for each house, and separate the services. The difference between our proposed subdivision costs and the actual costs were caused by the type of driveway the council required.

Difficult tenants

We had some problems managing the tenants. I think I have seen the worst of tenants already. (But maybe not.) One of them just ran off, breaking her lease. (We had to apply to the tribunal and recover her rent and losses before finding another one.) The other was a very difficult tenant and overstayed the lease period. We had to apply to the tribunal again, but she moved out a few weeks later.

We needed to communicate right from the start that they would be short-term tenants and we needed them to vacate once the lease expired. I think they expected to stay there for a longer period.

We've learnt from this how important it is to select good tenants. We now know that if you choose your tenants poorly, you waste a lot of time managing them, and lose money when they damage the property or break the lease.

Table 8.1: real deal figures

	Proposed	Actual numbers at the time of writing
Purchase price	$485 000	$485 000
Closing costs	$20 000	$20 000
Holding costs	$0 (cash flow neutral)	$0*
Subdivision costs	$95 000	$120 000 (including applications, construction and project management)
Total costs	*$600 000*	*$625 000*
Sale front house	$350 000	$420 000
Sale back house	$350 000	$430 000 (estimated)
Sale costs	$22 000	$22 000
Length of project	12 months	15 months
Profit	**$78 000**	**$203 000**

* Positively geared net rental income of approximately $5000 from $100 per week for one year. This has been ignored in these calculations.

On the road to financial freedom...

Treat tenants as if they are partners in your wealth creation – because they are! It's vital that you treat them well if you want things to run smoothly; don't see them simply as a hassle in the investment process.

So far, so good...

The deal is currently going according to plan. We got the subdivision approval. We are in the construction phase for the next six weeks. Our numbers and timing were very conservative and we used the worst case scenarios in our preparation, so now the numbers actually look better. There were a few hiccups with the tenants but we managed to work around that so it didn't affect our final numbers. It's been a great learning process.

We sold the front property for $70 000 more than we planned. Our initial estimate was conservative because I had no similar deals to compare on a battleaxe block (a block with one house on the front and one at the back, with the driveway for the back house going down the side of the front house). We also happened to be holding the property during a boom in prices in Sydney, so that also added to our sale price. Some people might see this as being lucky, but I consider it a result of our hard work. I found a good deal and was in the market at the right time. This property was on the market for eight months before we bought it, so there was plenty of opportunity for somebody else to take on this deal.

During my due diligence I got to know almost every agent in the area and had classified them into buying and selling agents. I decided on one real estate agent to be my future selling agent, having seen him at many open houses. Not surprisingly, he has been the most proactive person in my team. We made a plan and he found a buyer for me for the front house from his network just before the construction started, for a sale off the plan. We got an offer, he negotiated to get it into the price bracket we were happy with and we exchanged contracts. We think we might be able to sell the back property for $430 000, because of the price we achieved for the front house. This would give us a total profit of more than $200 000.

Finding the ideal property for renovating and subdividing

Initially I was looking to buy a property, knock down the existing house, build a duplex, subdivide and then sell the two properties separately. I was looking for an older, rundown house (to keep the purchase price down) on at least 600 square metres of land with a frontage of at least 15 metres, preferably on a corner block. Having the property slope down towards the road is ideal so that there are no drainage problems. And I would be aiming for a sell price of around $450 000 for each property. You can see that I had quite specific requirements.

This deal met most of my needs, except that there were already two separate houses on the block. Rather than being a problem, this was an unexpected bonus. During my research on this property I found a clause in the council rules that suggested it would be easier to subdivide a property that already has two separate houses on it. This showed me how important it is to educate yourself about all areas of property. An obscure clause in the council rules made a big difference to this deal. If I didn't know about this I wouldn't have known the true value of this deal.

I have learnt that while it is very important to have a detailed description of the type of property you are looking for, it's also important to be flexible and adapt your deal if an opportunity presents itself. I did so, and it worked out extremely well. I crunched the numbers to work out the best option.

Finding the confidence

Initially I was struggling to come out of my comfort zone to venture into this completely new field. But just getting started and researching regularly, increasing my knowledge, speaking with my Property Coach often and asking possibly silly questions built my knowledge and confidence. I think I am handling everything surprisingly well. I am working on things within my control so everything is progressing according to plan.

I am in touch with my solicitor and rental manager often and am using my team to my advantage. Knowing the legal requirements has been important, and being pragmatic and getting my investor hat on to work out how to minimise my losses and making the negative work to my advantage is helping.

I researched my target area for many different strategies, including duplex development, for around five to six months before I found this one. It sat on the market for around eight months, and I had been looking at it as being an interesting possibility but was still researching other deals. Finally I realised its potential, concentrated on it and for one and a half months did further due diligence on it. This included endless hours of talks with the council, surveyors and real estate agents.

But even then I was still in doubt, until my Property Coach pointed out that I was overdoing the due diligence and asking questions even the council couldn't answer. I had gained access to documents from the council's archives that even the vendor didn't have after living there for 50 years!

Finally I let go, and we signed our first contract! Looking back, it was one of my 'aha' moments. Learning as I go has been part of the process and made me more confident. I think I am much better now at anticipating and handling problems than I ever was.

> **On the road to financial freedom...**
>
> There is such a thing as too much due diligence. If you're waiting for that piece of information that will tell you this deal is definitely going to succeed, you'll be waiting a long time. There is an element of risk even for the most diligent and well-prepared investor. Sooner or later you must dive in.

My tips for other investors

My tips for other investors starting out in property are:

➤ It's not about bricks and mortar as I initially thought. It's about people and managing them.

➤ Having a good mentor can save a lot of time and effort as well as keep you accountable.

➤ Create space in your life for educating yourself.

➤ Get out there and do it! (This was the hardest part for me, but once you get to the other end you are no longer the same person.)

My current situation

I am self-employed at the moment. I have scheduled one day a week for my part-time job and two days for my property business. The rest of the time I am a full-time mother and a housewife; however, that can change depending on what my priority is for that week. I intend to devote four days a week next year to property when my son is in school full time.

Looking to the future

I am looking into being a more or less full-time property developer. The success of my first deal has given me the confidence to try more creative deals. I am working on building my team and looking into further subdivision and development opportunities in the form of a joint venture deal. I am expanding my knowledge base and increasing my understanding of the concept of being an entrepreneur.

To us financial freedom means generating a passive income from our investments which will fund our lifestyles. So we don't devote all our energy to our day jobs but rather have the freedom to choose how we actually use all this energy and potential when we are still young for the betterment of ourselves and people around us. Our goal is to achieve financial freedom in five years; we are on track to do so and feel it is achievable, and we are very excited about it!

🏠 🏠 🏠

Shilpa was a little reluctant when she first ventured into property, but she overcame her doubts and persevered. And now she's working on this great deal! It's normal to be a bit hesitant when venturing into a new field. Don't let this put you off. All the people in this book felt the same way at some stage, but they kept going and are now experiencing great success.

Do something!

By this stage you should have an idea of your financial position, your strengths and the strategy you have in mind, and have come up with your ideal numbers for that strategy. Now it's time to describe the property you want to buy. In this description, include the following:

- the purchase price

- a list of suburbs you are considering exploring

- the size of land

Do something! *(Cont'd)*

- the type and style of house

- the number of bedrooms, bathrooms and living rooms

- the add-value costs for an add-value project or the holding costs for a rental

- the proposed selling price or rental return.

Bonus content

To hear Shilpa speak about her deal in more detail, go to <www.resultsmentoring.com/book1/>.

Chapter 9

Separating and renovating a duplex

We have looked at how much you can afford to spend on a property and where you could look to buy. The next step is to establish your criteria for an ideal property for your type of deal.

Finding your ideal property

If you know the desirable property criteria for your strategy, you can make a decision as to whether a property warrants further investigation.

For example, if your chosen strategy is cosmetic renovation, you want to find a house that is structurally sound in a layout that can be modified slightly to create a more modern feel without any structural work.

Hands on, lump-sum cash/equity

Separating and renovating a duplex

(Chart: vertical axis "Costs" with Low, Medium, High; horizontal axis "Complexity/risk" with Low, Medium, High; a shaded oval positioned at High costs / Medium–High complexity/risk)

Cash/equity requirements

- Medium amount of money required for a deposit and closing (settlement) costs, depending upon property purchase price
- Medium amount of additional money required to fund the reno and the subdivision
- Medium amount of money required each month to service the loan repayments (potentially offset by any rent received)

Borrowing capacity requirements

- Typically medium debt-servicing levels relative to the price of the dwelling

Complexity/risk

- Medium complexity, medium risk for lump-sum cash profit

Skills requirements

- Medium/high levels of researching, due diligence, area and deal analysis and negotiation skills will be required
- Medium/high levels of project management and people skills will be required
- Medium/high handyman skills and knowledge of house construction if DIY

Time requirements

- Medium/high amounts of time needed to find, analyse, negotiate and buy property
- Medium/high amounts of time required to execute the reno and subdivide the property (highest if DIY)
- The time required to complete and on-sell the project is typically nine to 12 months

Desired outcome

- Cash lump-sum profit or equity gain

It's probably going to be a house built in the 1960s, 1970s or 1980s that has never had anything done to improve it (older houses increase the risk of hidden structural issues). And — as we have seen — your ideal property is likely to be in an area where there is a 33 per cent price differential between unrenovated properties and renovated properties, and where renovated properties have a track record of good sales.

This is only a broad description of the type of property you might look for. Using this as your starting point, you then need to understand what the target market is in that area and what that target market wants. This becomes part of the due diligence for your deal. For example, is it more profitable to on-sell your property to an owner-occupier or to an investor for a rental return?

Answering questions like this will allow you to further narrow down the criteria for your ideal property. The more specific you are, the easier it will be to make a decision about a property, and the way in which you might choose to renovate it.

The reason for creating an ideal property description is so that you can search very quickly for properties that are going to give you the outcome you desire in the right area. If your strategy is cosmetic renovation and a real estate agent comes to you with a recently constructed four-bedroom house on a very large block and asks if you want to buy it, you could answer 'no' straight away. If an agent offers you a two-bedroom unit in a new apartment block the answer is also 'no'. You can eliminate unsuitable properties very quickly because you know exactly what you are looking for.

Hitting the street

So far we've talked about the importance of understanding why you're investing and your financial position; choosing a strategy based on your skills, available cash, strengths, desired outcome and passions; and knowing your numbers. We've also looked at finding your ideal property and the 15-minute suburb search, so now you know what you're after and where to look. Now's the time for you to get in the car, drive the streets and talk to real estate agents!

Have a look at <www.realestate.com.au> or <www.real estate.co.nz> and start to look for properties that match your ideal property description that are in suburbs that meet your criteria and match your desired purchase price. If you've done your homework and your numbers well, you should be able to find one or two of these properties.

Now phone the relevant agents and ask them about the property. (If you need some help with this, in chapter 10 there are some questions to ask agents.) Your aim is to start building a rapport with the agents.

Why do you want to do this?

A great way to find out about properties before anybody else does is to get to the top of agents' buyers lists, and to do this you have to build a good relationship with them. Remember Troy S in chapter 6? He built a strong relationship with an agent, and as a result he was told about the property in his deal before it was even advertised! A good relationship with an agent may also help you negotiate reasonable prices.

Agents' lists

Real estate agents basically have two lists that they work from: houses for sale, and buyers who want them. Let's have a look at these.

Houses for sale

It's an agent's job to get listings to sell properties, and they are in competition with other agents to do this. When a seller agrees to list with an agent, they will sign a listing agreement. The most common type of listing agreement is an 'exclusivity agreement', where the vendor is obligated to pay the agent a commission if the property sells through anybody at any point during the agreement. You can also have a general listing agreement where more than one agency will list your property and the commission is paid to whoever makes the sale.

Most listing agreements last 90 days (about 12 weeks), which makes choosing the right agent of critical importance for sellers. This is because agents think that they are likely to find a buyer for most properties within 90 days. A listing agreement that includes an auction is generally made up of 30 days of advertising, the auction day, and then 60 days after if the property doesn't sell.

On the road to financial freedom...

When you are selling, try to get a listing for six weeks rather than 12. Most sales occur in the first six weeks of a listing, when interest in the property is high. If you don't sell after six weeks, you can then move to another agent and generate renewed hype around the property.

Buyers lists

Your role as a serious investor is to get on agents' buyers lists. You can do this by being committed, cashed up and ready to buy. Once you are on the list, buying once or twice a year from that agent will keep you on the list. And when you prove to be a good client, the agents will start to call you!

For agents it's not too hard to tell if you are a serious investor. Don't start your conversation with an agent by saying: 'Hi, I'm looking to buy a property to make some money'. The agent will probably reply, 'Yeah, you and everybody else!' You want to come across as a serious investor, not a try-hard. If you don't give the agent any information to help them find the property you are after, they will know you have not done any preparation and are not likely to be ready to buy. They might feel you are just going to waste their time.

To get their time and attention, you might consider approaching agents with something like this: 'I'm looking for a property on about 800 square metres with the house on the front left corner of the property. It has three bedrooms and two bathrooms, in a solid but tired state, preferably brick with a tiled roof. A low front fence would be nice, and I don't care if the lawn hasn't been mowed for weeks. If it's smelly and old it's even better. Have you got anything like that on your books?'

Of course the details of the property will be specific to your situation, but you can see the level of detail in this description. This is what you have to do to demonstrate to agents that you are a serious, well-prepared investor and not just a 'tyre kicker'. Agents will then treat you differently because you know what you want and will be more likely to buy from them.

If you call the agent back a few days after your enquiry they may not remember you, but if you call every Monday for six weeks they will! Contact agents regularly with genuine enquiries and they will know you are serious and remember who you are.

On the road to financial freedom...

Befriend one agent at every agency. Call this person regularly, and keep track of their listings. When they complete a good sale, say to them, 'I saw in the paper you sold that property', and congratulate them. This will help to establish a relationship.

If you stay in regular contact with an agent, make genuine enquiries, show interest in them, discuss your projects with them and act like a professional investor, you can work your way up the list. You get to number 1 by having your chequebook ready when they find the right property for you.

If you want to rapidly disappear from an agent's list, keep saying 'no' to deals they offer you without giving them a good reason. They will stop calling you very soon.

Networking

Networking is an important part of successful investing. Agents will become a part of your network, but it's also a great idea for you to be in regular contact with like-minded people who are also out there making property deals. You may not meet many of these people in your everyday life, so it's important to make an effort to find them.

There are many different types of investing groups and organisations around the country that you can join. For example, propertymeeting.com.au, which has information about property investing meetings around Australia, and Active Property Network <www.activepropertynetwork.com.au>, which was set up to support like-minded property investors in Melbourne. These groups meet at least once a month to support and encourage each other, and to share stories and information. Such groups are a great way to meet up with people who are on the same journey as you.

🛒 🛒 🛒

Now let's meet David—his real deal is the renovation and subdivision of an existing duplex. Look for how David described the ideal property for his deal.

Real deal: renovating and subdividing a duplex

Hi, my name is David. I'm 43 years old. I was an engineer in an automotive company three or four years ago, and I'm married with a couple of kids. My four year old is a budding builder—after seeing me working on the kitchen renovation at our house, he decided his bedroom could do with some work so he took to it with a screwdriver!

A few years ago I was in a job I didn't like, and I was wondering what other options I had. I came to property investing after a conversation I had with a supplier. This person was doing exceptionally well financially and he had a lot of free time, so I asked him what his secret was. His answer: property investing!

I didn't know much about property at this time. I had owned a couple of negatively geared properties, but this was the limit of my experience. I had even sold one of these for less than I paid for it because the management process became too difficult. That wasn't a particularly successful deal.

My strategy

My initial property strategy was renovation. I did a couple of those early on in my investing career, but I came to the conclusion that they can be very labour intensive and so I wanted to change my tactics a little bit.

I was looking around my target area, which I knew quite well, and saw that there were quite a few duplex properties; that is, two units on one title sitting on about 600 square metres of land. There weren't too many people demanding that sort of property, so there was an excess in supply, but there were plenty of people in this area who could afford to buy a two-bedroom unit on its own title. I saw an opportunity to subdivide these units and on-sell them individually, and so that became my strategy.

My ideal property

The ideal property I was after was a block with a small rundown duplex or co-joined dwelling on it. Ideally it would appeal to a low-end market or an investor who wants to buy a neat low-end property. I wanted a smallish block because I believed my end user was not going to want a lot of maintenance. I also wanted to be able to create private open space to attract buyers, or attract tenants so that an investor could achieve a higher rent.

I was looking for as much of the necessary infrastructure to be in place as possible, such as separate water and electricity meters and the dividing wall going from the ground to the roof. Separate driveways with carports or garages would be ideal so that I wouldn't need to put them in.

So I felt I had to be very specific. My ideal properties had to have:

> street frontage for each unit

> a driveway for each unit

> separate meters for electricity, water and gas for each unit

> separate backyards

> land of about 600 square metres

> a double-brick dividing wall that went all the way down to ground level and all the way up to the bottom of the roof tiles, for fire safety.

Once I knew exactly what I was looking for, the process of finding good properties for my strategy became less labour intensive and relatively easy. I could look at a property and if it didn't meet my criteria I would straight away move on to the next one.

Having a clear idea of my ideal property also allowed me to expand my search area when looking for properties. I eventually ended up researching and looking for these properties up to 300 kilometres away from where I initially started looking.

Found one!

The property I purchased for this deal was a duplex on 720 square metres, which is slightly bigger than my ideal property but in this case the larger size would generate a slightly better profit. It was a typical 1970s cream-brick property, with a couple of two-bedroom units sharing a common wall with separate driveways. It was separately metered for power, water and gas, and had the fire-rated wall that I desired. I secured the property at an acceptable price after some negotiations with the vendor.

Initially this deal was just going to be a get in, subdivide, get out over six months. I had negotiated a six-month settlement on this property so the plan was to complete the subdivision in this time, so that I didn't have any holding costs.

However, the project ended up taking 12 months. With the introduction of the First Home Owner Grant this type of property became more desirable, and so the decision was made to renovate the properties and then sell them, rather than just subdividing and selling them in their current state. We also thought we would be able to sell them a lot quicker if they were renovated. In the area there weren't too many well-presented two-bedroom units, but there was a high demand for this type of property.

I only did cosmetic work on the units, not structural work (figure 9.1 shows some before and after pictures). I put in new kitchens, but they were very basic. I left the existing fittings in the bathrooms; I just re-enamelled the bath and shower and put in new tiles. I polished the floorboards throughout and painted the walls. That's about it!

On the road to financial freedom...

If you are considering doing the reno work yourself, don't forget to factor in the cost of tools. To get the job done properly you will need professional equipment; this can be very expensive, and can negate some or all of the benefit of doing the work yourself.

Figure 9.1: the property before and after

A minor problem

I employed a land surveyor to survey the land and submit my application to subdivide to the council. In response the council said that they would like the buildings to comply with the current building regulations, so I also needed a building surveyor report stating that they did. I contacted two building surveyors, and it turned out that such a report was going to cost around $25000! This was a bit of concern—that would wipe out my expected profit on the deal.

I explained the situation to my land surveyor, and he put me in touch with a building surveyor that he knew. This surveyor said that the council was really only concerned about the buildings meeting fire regulations, and he could do a report on this for $2000. This satisfied the council—and me—and the subdivision was approved.

> **On the road to financial freedom ...**
>
> Don't take the first quote as final. If a price seems unreasonable, investigate further to see if the price is justified. You can always get another quote.

Sold!

I didn't have any problems selling the units once work was complete. The first one sold for $210000 and the second for $235000. The difference between the selling prices was because the first unit was renovated in a short space of time and put straight back on the market. The second unit was sold 12 months later, and prices had increased in this time.

The figures

The figures for the deal are shown in table 9.1.

Table 9.1: real deal figures

Purchase price	$300250
Closing costs	$15000
Time	12 months
Holding costs	$6000
Reno costs	$20000
Subdivision costs	$5000
Selling costs	$12000
Sale price	
Unit 1:	$210000
Unit 2:	$235000
Total:	$445000
Profit	**$86750**

You may wonder about that unusual buy price. I had been following this property in the lead-up to the auction and going to the inspections each time it was open. Three days before the auction was due to take place, the agent rang me and said the vendor didn't want to go to auction and instead would accept offers over $300 000—so I offered $300 250! Seemed logical to me. The agent had a bit of a laugh and said he didn't think this would get it done, but he took the offer to the vendor. And it was accepted! A day before the auction had been scheduled to take place, I was the new owner of the property.

My initial profit expectation for this deal was $25 000, but the change of approach (doing the reno) produced more than triple this profit. It was a great result, and it goes to show that changing your plan once a project is underway can be beneficial as long as you know what direction you want to head and the numbers tell you it's a good idea.

On the road to financial freedom...

Always have a plan, but if a new opportunity presents itself mid-project look for ways to adapt your approach to maximise your profits.

Tips for new investors

My tips for new investors are:

➤   If you want to be a serious investor, be serious about your investing and treat it like a business. Real estate agents, surveyors, builders and other people you have to deal with will treat you like a professional if you look and behave like one.

➤   You make your profit in knowing the numbers before you buy.

➤   Don't forget to celebrate your achievements.

My current situation

I am now a full-time property investor enjoying a much more satisfying life and I'm on the road to financial freedom. I think I'll get there in three years, or perhaps a bit earlier with some hard work. I'm very excited about this.

The reason I do what I do is to enable me to buy back my time. I spent seven weeks prior to the above project touring the east coast of Australia with my family.

I no longer have to answer to a boss, and I'm able to spend much more time with my family and have greater control over my life.

I'm currently planning to do a land subdivision for my next property deal.

Looking to the future

My short-term goal is to return to the east coast of Australia but extend the time to 12 weeks. My company will also turn over approximately $1.8 million in property with a profit margin of between 12 per cent and 14 per cent.

My long-term goal is to develop a property portfolio of positive cash flow properties in high-growth areas. This may sound impossible to some people, but as I complete more successful deals over the next five years I believe it will become a reality.

🏠 🏠 🏠

David's result is outstanding. He made $86 000 on this deal as a direct result of carrying out sound area and deal analysis, and diligently managing the project through to completion. There's no reason why you can't do similar. Create a clear description of your ideal property, and then get out there to find it.

Do something!

It's now time to create a detailed description of the ideal property you're seeking. Write it down on paper and keep it near the computer for when you do your internet searching.

Bonus content

To hear David speak about his deal in more detail, go to <www.resultsmentoring.com/book1/>.

Chapter 10

Renovate and subdivide (1 into 2)

As you may have noticed already, it is possible to combine different property strategies in a single deal. You can renovate a positive cash flow property, you can subdivide and then develop a block, you can subdivide and then hold for the long term; in fact, the possibilities are almost endless. If the numbers tell you it's a good idea, you can combine strategies in whatever way you wish.

In this chapter we're going to hear from Colleen. Her strategy for this particular deal was to combine renovation and subdivision. There is nothing too complicated about doing a deal such as this. It will of course be more involved than doing just one or the other, and your due diligence must be thorough and comprehensive.

Hands on, lump-sum cash/equity

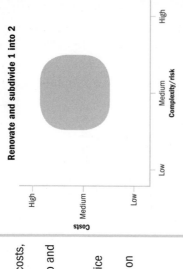

Renovate and subdivide 1 into 2

(Chart: Costs axis — High, Medium, Low; Complexity/risk axis — Low, Medium, High)

Cash/equity requirements

- Medium/high amount of money required for a deposit and closing costs, depending upon property purchase price
- Medium/high amount of additional money required to fund the reno and the subdivision

Borrowing capacity requirements

- Medium/high amount of borrowing dependent upon the size and price of a property big enough to subdivide
- Medium amount of money required each month to service the debt on the vacant property while the reno is being completed

Complexity/risk

- Medium complexity, medium risk for lump-sum cash profit

Skills requirements

- Medium/high levels of researching, area and deal analysis and negotiation skills will be required
- Medium/high levels of project management and people skills will be required
- Medium handyman skills and knowledge of house construction if DIY reno
- High levels of patience (for dealing with local authorities)

Time requirements

- Medium/high time will be needed to find, analyse, negotiate and buy property
- Medium/high time will be required to execute the reno
- Low time required for the subdivision, as most day-to-day tasks are outsourced

Desired outcome

- Cash lump-sum profit upon sale of house and separate land

At this point in the book we have explored with you why you want to invest, goal setting and the need for budgets and financial control (chapter 1), the set of skills, time, cash and borrowing capacity you have at your disposal (chapters 2 and 3), your need to consider the market that you are investing into (chapter 4), choosing your strategy (chapter 5), doing the numbers and beginning to look at areas to find your deal (chapter 6), an example of how to narrow your search (chapter 7) into your ideal property (chapters 8 and 9). Now it's time to actually look at the process of buying a property and what you will need to make a sound purchasing decision.

> **On the road to financial freedom...**
>
> Why would you do a renovation and a subdivision? For the same reason that you would choose any investing strategy: your analysis tells you that this will be the most profitable option.

Buying property

Let's have a look at some of the issues you must consider when buying a property.

Buying a problem

You may be surprised to hear this, but when you are buying a property you should look to buy a *problem*. Buying a problem means buying an opportunity. If you can solve the problem, you may have created a solution that you can sell for a profit.

You will notice that many of the investors in this book bought properties that at first might not have seemed very attractive, perhaps because there was a lot of work involved. But this is where the opportunity lies: if you do the work that others are unwilling to take on, you will likely be rewarded. For example, you might buy a run-down property to live in for $250000, renovate it over 12 months and sell it to a buy and hold investor for $390000, making a profit on the way. The buy and hold investor will most likely make a profit too, but will have to hold the house for a number of years and rely on market growth to do so. In buying the run-down property and fixing it up you have created your own profit and solved the problem for the buy and hold investor who wanted to own such a property but didn't want to undertake the reno. Another example of solving a problem is subdividing property in an area where there is a housing shortage, or building a block of units for student accommodation near a university. Always consider the problem when you are seeking out deals. Problems equal potential profit!

Some questions to ask real estate agents

Dealing with real estate agents can be daunting if you are new to property and looking to buy. When you start out they know more about property than you do. As they are on the side of the seller, they may try to take advantage of your inexperience. Even as you gain confidence, some agents are expert negotiators who may try to get the best of you if you are unprepared.

To help you in your dealings with agents when buying, here are some questions you might want to ask. This list is a guide only, and you should ask as many questions as you can of the agent to extract the information you need. Remember the agent is on the vendor's side, not yours, so many will try to put a positive spin on their answers.

On the road to financial freedom ...

Be reasonable when dealing with agents and vendors. You should always try to get the best price you can, but don't risk a good deal trying to squeeze every last dollar out of the vendor. If the price is reasonable and the figures look good, seal the deal.

What is the asking price?
Simple! This will get the discussion rolling.

How did the vendor come up with this price?
Most buyers don't ask this question, so it will get the agent's attention. This will help you to establish how much room there is to negotiate. If the vendor has set the price based on paying off a mortgage or buying another property, for example, there might be less room to move. If the agent simply says 'That's the market', the price has probably been set by the agent and there might be more room to negotiate.

Is the price negotiable?
This is basically asking if you can submit an offer lower than the asking price. Of course you don't actually need to ask to do this, but this question will help you establish the ground rules for the negotiation. If the agents says no, the next question should be, why not?

Why is the vendor selling? Is the vendor keen for a quick sale?
This will help you establish what terms might be required for the vendor to accept your offer.

How long has the property been on the market?
If the property has been on the market for a long time, it means either the vendor will be getting anxious to sell and there might be more flexibility, or time is not an issue and the vendor is holding out for the 'right' price.

What was the original listing price? What offers have there been so far?
This will help you establish the parameters within which you can negotiate. You can also ask why the previous offers fell through.

What are the terms of sale? Are they flexible?
Although price is usually the biggest consideration for most people, you must also take the terms of sale into account. Two important terms are the amount of deposit required and the

settlement period, and there can be many others. The terms of the agreement are negotiated as part of the deal. The vendor is usually flexible on either price or terms, very rarely both. The right terms can improve profitability.

Would I be able to get early access?
Getting access to the property before settlement can be a great help for some strategies, especially renovation. If you can get a head start, it might mean the project will be completed more quickly and you will save on holding costs. Don't expect to knock down walls, but taking measurements and obtaining quotes should be fine. You could also consider landscaping. Keep in mind though that you will need to pay for insurance on the property for this period.

On the road to financial freedom...

Make sure that any conditions you negotiate are included in the contract. Have this confirmed by your lawyer.

Would the vendor provide a discount for a cash offer?
An unconditional cash offer can get you a substantial discount if the vendor is in a hurry to sell. But there are risks! You *must* have the ability to finance the deal, and be confident in your due diligence. In making such an offer you are basically removing any protections you might have so that you can get a lower price, so be 100 per cent sure you know what you are doing!

What are the growth prospects for this sort of property in this area?
The agent is of course going to say 'Fantastic!' This is not the information you are after. What you are looking to do is start a conversation with the agent about what's happening in the area, to see what you can find out to help you make a better buying decision about the property.

Have you sold any similar properties in the area recently? What did they sell for?
The answers to these questions will help you to establish what the current market is for this area, and also how often similar properties are selling.

How do you think this property's value could be improved?
This gives you the opportunity to get some ideas from somebody who is in touch with buyers on a daily basis. An agent should have good knowledge about what buyers expect for their money in the area.

On the road to financial freedom ...

Even if a deal you are discussing with the agent doesn't proceed you can gain valuable information to help you with future deals, so always find out as much as you can.

If you decide not to proceed with a deal always tell the agent why. This will help you retain credibility with the agent and may even lead to other opportunities as the agent gets a better idea of what you are looking for.

Find your most profitable exit

Before you get into a deal, you must have a detailed plan for when you are going to get out. If you haven't decided when you are going to sell, how can you calculate the potential profit on the deal? And if you haven't calculated the potential profit on the deal, of course you wouldn't be buying, would you?

Your exit plan should clearly outline what work needs to be done before the deal is considered complete. You can even consider different exit points for your deal and calculate the profit on each. What matters most is that your exit plan matches the strategy you have chosen. For example, if you are looking at a vacant lot with the aim of building and subdividing, but your figures show the best profit is to be made subdividing the block and selling as vacant land, you will either need to reassess your strategy or find a different property. Some deals will present you with numerous possible exit points; it's up to you to decide which one to take.

Contingency plans

It's also very important to have contingency plans in place before you start on the deal. Sometimes your most profitable exit strategy won't work due to unforeseen circumstances, so you must have a plan B (and sometimes a plan C) and be prepared to go down a different path if things don't go as expected.

You must also know what the triggers are for initiating your plan B. For example, if you are undertaking a construction deal and the market turns against you after you have bought the property and started planning, what will you do? In such a situation it might be best to sell the property with plans and permits. This might result in a loss on the deal, but a small loss now is better than a larger loss later. To sell the property with plans and approvals now and lose $50 000 is better than completing the construction but then losing $400 000!

🛒 🛒 🛒

Now we're going to hear from Colleen. She saw a property on the internet one night and bought it the next day! She was able to do this because she had already decided on her strategy and crunched her numbers, and this property matched what she was looking for.

Let's see how this deal turned out.

Real deal: subdividing into two lots

Hello, I'm Colleen. I worked as a midwife up until we had our second child. My husband has been and remains a teacher at a local private school, which he enjoys. I have since had a third child and wanted to stay at home with my children.

We have a number of reasons for getting into real estate investing, mostly cash. Weekend shifts could have been an option, but I needed to babysit the children when my husband played cricket on Saturdays, we attend church as a family on Sundays and the rest was family time.

We see value in sending our children through the private schooling system and would be unable to achieve this just on Stuart's income alone, and even if I worked part time it would be a struggle. We would also like to share some great travel experiences as a family overseas in countries that are remarkably different to ours. Another significant motivation is to be able to make a difference in other people's lives, not just financially but also with time.

We knew and spoke with other people who were investing in property with success and felt it was an avenue we could understand and thought that it was a 'safer' option. We decided that this might be a way for me to earn an income while staying at home with the kids.

We had a little bit of investing experience. We had our own home and bought our first investment property, a rooming/share house, in 2006 prior to commencing the program in 2007. This ended up being a long 14-month settlement as we waited for the vendor to have the back part of the property subdivided and put on separate titles before we could take possession. We then increased the value of the property by increasing its return with more occupancy, from four tenants to five. The market also went up slightly during the settlement period. We held the property for about six months, then sold with a profit, after all costs, just short of $50 000. When we decided to make a real go of property we found a mentor to help us.

> **On the road to financial freedom...**
>
> Property investing is not a race. Don't rush into any deals just because you think you need to get going quickly. Go into a deal when the numbers tell you to, and not a moment before.

Why we chose renovate and subdivide

We chose this hands-on strategy because we felt with the subdivision as well as the renovation there would be more opportunity to make better profits, yet it was less scary than development. We had previously done a small renovation on our home, but that was it. We decided we wanted cash lump-sum deals so that we could grow our capital reasonably quickly, as opposed to holding onto property and relying solely on capital growth in the market place.

I wanted a property over a certain land size, which varies depending on the area, zoning and requirements of the council. The house has to then be in a position that will allow enough access down the side of the property (different for a corner block) and obviously enough backyard/sideyard available to create a new piece of land after private open space and car parking has been considered for the existing property. I like houses that are solid though cosmetically challenged. The property in this deal suited my criteria well.

Buying

In mid 2008 I found a house on <www.realestate.com.au> on a 1017-square-metre corner block in the outer eastern suburbs of Melbourne. It was a standard brick veneer, neat and structurally sound. I was attracted to it because of its land size and it was a reasonably ordinary house with potential to improve. I calculated the figures on the property and did my research and it looked like a good deal, so I bought it. My plan for this property was to subdivide into two lots, cosmetically renovate the house, then sell the lot with the house and sell the other parcel of land once it was subdivided with its own street frontage.

I bought the property at auction after seeing it for the first time on the internet the night before. I had done the numbers on the property the night before and felt there was not a lot of profit in the deal based on my expectations of what it would sell for; however, I thought I would check it out anyway along with others I had on my list for that day. Our finances were already in order. Our mortgage broker had worked out our borrowing capacity and ability to repay based on my husband Stuart's income. We have no debts, low credit card limits and pay our credit card off monthly if we use it.

I would have seen close to 100 properties with the same strategy in mind, and made five or six offers that had been rejected. By now I knew what to look for, so I checked for any obvious defects that I could see with the naked eye (although that's a risk without a building inspection), stepped out the land and read and re-read the contract for sale. It wasn't until I spoke to one of the agents prior to the auction that I thought this could be a possibility. She mentioned they had prior offers that were about $80000 less than what I thought it would sell for. There was only one other bidder, who stopped early on, and the property was passed in to me. It was so helpful to know my numbers to keep most emotion out of the game. One of the agents after I signed called me a 'hard woman'. I was kind of proud of this because if you knew me it is not my character. It's all about the numbers! Also I thought it was a case of preparation meeting opportunity.

> **On the road to financial freedom...**
>
> It can be a good strategy to be flexible on terms or price, but not both. This won't always be possible, but give it a try when you can.

An ordinary house with potential to improve

The renovation included painting the whole interior, polishing floorboards, adding new window furnishings, adding new carpet to the large sunroom, and putting in a new outside deck and a modern sliding door to access it. Painting tiles in the laundry and kitchen made a huge difference. Also the backyard was a complete mess so needed to be transformed. An existing double carport and shed were demolished to enable us to subdivide, and there were no overlays on the property so we were able to clear most of the block. We had another carport and crossover (driveway) built for the existing house on the opposite side.

We also completely renovated the bathroom, which wasn't part of the original plan. I had discussed with several real estate agents the value of adding an extra toilet which could fit in the bathroom, and the wall tiles were also warped. We decided that fixing up the bathroom would add more in perceived value than actual cost and was therefore worth doing.

A big turn-off when I bought the property was the over-whelming stench of cigarette smoke that was present throughout the house. You could even smell the smoke from the street. I felt physically sick and had to have a shower after each time I visited. We fixed most of this by pulling the carpet up.

> **On the road to financial freedom...**
>
> You can find out about overlays on a property by reading the contract for sale and contacting the council.

Anyone for a swim?

There was a swimming pool on the block which the council wanted us to fill in. We had spoken to several real estate agents about the end sale price on land with a pool as opposed to a completely vacant block. It would have cost us up to $15 000 to fill the pool in, with supposedly little difference in the end sale result. The problem was that council was opposed to having a pool on a vacant block even with a fence around it: given that no one would be residing there they saw it as too dangerous. So I asked a different question to council: was there any way that the pool could remain, and had anyone done this before? Apparently 20 years ago someone had the same issue and the council agreed for him to put a solid timber roof directly above the pool as well as a temporary surrounding fence. This was what I ended up being able to do as well. It pays to ask a different question.

Meeting the neighbours

We had applied to and been approved by the council for a two-storey residence to be built on the vacant land. The neighbour next door complained about the building envelope (this is the footprint that the building would make on the land) and applied to the tribunal to oppose the plan the council had approved. However, fortunately after my Property Mentor and I contacted the resident we were able to negotiate some changes that pleased both of us. We placed some minor conditions on the two-storey building to be built, such as upper storey set back and height of windows, and thankfully he then withdrew his complaint. A tribunal hearing would have set us back a couple of months on our project, which of course would mean more interest and holding costs for the property.

Time to sell

The property was marketed to first home buyers through the real estate agent I had chosen and knew I'd work well with.

The deal worked out far above our expectations. I was very conservative in my initial numbers with my estimated end sales prices for the completed house and separate land once subdivided. Then the cream on top was the competition provided by the vast number of first home buyers looking at our property. We'd obviously got the marketing right.

When selling I believe we got the best price by knowing our target market, by staging the property and having great photos taken, by choosing an agent that would work really hard and well with us and for us, with great follow up and negotiation skills. I had an active part to play in the copywriting with help from my Property Mentor.

I have sold properties via auction and private sale; my choice, in discussion with my agent, has depended on the property we are selling, what the market is doing at the time and the target market.

The figures

You can see from the figures in table 10.1 that this was a very good deal for us.

For this deal we were able to achieve $0 in holding costs because we sold the home we were living in and put this cash towards the deal, so there were no interest costs. We ended up spending a bit more than we had originally planned on the renovation, but this resulted in a higher selling cost so it wasn't a problem.

Our property team

I have found if I am going to be serious about investing I need a team of people around me to make it all work. I realise now it's not something I can do on my own. Over time I've developed a team of advisers and support. In my team I have a solicitor, mortgage broker and accountant who were recommended to us. Our builder and plumber are reliable friends, and other tradesmen were found based on price and availability. Some of the tradesmen I will use again, others I will not, so in some ways I am still building my team. The real estate agent I used was the one who sold our principal place of residence. But even though I felt he had done a good job and communicated well, I still did interviews with three other agents since this property was in a different area.

Table 10.1: real deal figures

Purchase price	$366 000
Closing costs	$19 000
Project length	12 months
Holding costs	$0
Subdivision costs	$23 000
Renovation costs	$39 000
Selling costs	$18 000
Sale price (house)	$388 000
Sale price (land)	$200 000
Profit	**$123 000**

Having a good team is essential for a smoother journey and to achieve success and we were fortunate to have had many of our team referred to us. In finding others we would ring around, ask lots of questions, try to find people we felt we could trust, people who have a positive 'can do' attitude (want to help you win), communicate with you, don't fob you off and want to work with you. It is important, however, that you also look after those in your team with appreciation, respect and quick payment.

Tips for new investors

My tips for investors starting out in property are:

➤ Have a good foundation of knowledge and do your research.

➤ Ask lots of questions. There are many experts out there in all sorts of areas who can help you.

➤ Clarity is so important in terms of being crystal clear about why you are doing what you are doing in order to keep you motivated, focused and give you purpose.

➤ Have a go!

My current situation

We sold our principal place of residence in 2007 as we had an amazing rental opportunity. It was a house that was bigger for our growing family, one street away from our home we sold, we knew the landlords and the rent was cheap. This would enable us to free up a lot of capital for investing, cater for our growing family and most months be able to save more from Stuart's income.

I'm still enjoying being at home with my children while investing in property, and now that I have some knowledge and experience behind me I feel I can take on more. One of our goals is to own our next home outright with enough money to continue to invest. We are not there yet and are quite happy renting in the meantime, as long as we are making our capital work for us. Stuart continues in his teaching role, which supplies cash flow for us, and is supportive of me focusing on the property investing

Looking to the future

We are currently doing a very similar subdivision deal on a much smaller block in a growth area. We have not decided to renovate at this stage — it may not be required as we may sell it for a good price without renovation once it is subdivided. We will rent it out this time while doing the plans for subdivision. We may even decide to hold this property once we've sold the land off, depending on what we sell the land for. It depends if the property will end up costing us anything to hold onto after rent. I am also looking for other properties at present so we are never without a property, especially in a growth market.

We want to make the most return on investment we can by maximising our loan-to-valuation ratio so our money is not being lazy. We will keep endeavouring to grow our capital through either turning over properties or keeping them if it doesn't cost us anything to do so and it is in a growth area. Our aim is to continually move forward with our investing and not get stuck where we can no longer afford to invest because of over-committing. We plan to buy one or two more properties this year — we came close to buying one just recently but we couldn't agree on conditions with the vendor. Our intention is to eventually hold some property for income.

To us financial freedom means having the lifestyle we want and concentrating on the things that mean the most to us. We would like to achieve financial freedom in 10 years.

🏠 🏠 🏠

Colleen's hard work and preparation paid off, and she's walked away with a very good profit. Well done Colleen!

Do something!

Go and talk to a real estate agent in the area you are looking to buy your next investment property. What information do you need to know to ensure that your next project will be a success? Think about some of the useful information that you would like to obtain from a real estate agent. Then make an appointment and go and have a chat.

Bonus content

To hear Colleen speak about her deal in more detail, go to <www.resultsmentoring.com/book1/>.

Chapter 11

Renovate and subdivide (1 into 3)

In this chapter we're going to hear about another renovate and subdivide deal. Steve and Mandy subdivided a single property with an existing house into three blocks. They then renovated the house and sold that lot, and left the other two vacant and sold them as well.

We're also going to keep building your team of experts to help and guide you. Read on!

Building your property team

To achieve ongoing investing success you will need to engage experts to help with your investing. Building a team that you can rely on is vital, and once you find a good and reliable expert make sure you maintain the relationship and stay in regular contact.

Hands on, lump-sum cash/equity

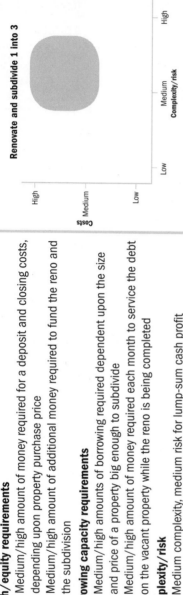

Renovate and subdivide 1 into 3

Cash/equity requirements

- Medium/high amount of money required for a deposit and closing costs, depending upon property purchase price
- Medium/high amount of additional money required to fund the reno and the subdivision

Borrowing capacity requirements

- Medium/high amounts of borrowing required dependent upon the size and price of a property big enough to subdivide
- Medium/high amount of money required each month to service the debt on the vacant property while the reno is being completed

Complexity/risk

- Medium complexity, medium risk for lump-sum cash profit

Skills requirements

- Medium/high levels of researching, area and deal analysis and negotiation skills will be required
- Medium/high levels of project management and people skills will be required
- Medium handyman skills and knowledge of house construction if DIY reno
- High levels of patience (for dealing with local authorities)

Time requirements

- Medium/high time will be needed to find, negotiate and buy property
- Medium/high time will be required to execute the reno
- Low time required for doing the subdivision as most day-to-day tasks are outsourced

Desired outcome

- Cash lump-sum profit upon sale of house and multiple blocks of land

Different strategies will require different experts—for example, you don't necessarily need a builder for a cosmetic reno. But there are experts that are essential for any type of deal—for example, lawyers and accountants.

Let's have a look at some of the different people who can help you with your investing:

➤ *Planning officers.* Most councils or planning authorities have a Planning Department that handles subdivision and development enquiries and applications. The planning officers can be very helpful if you develop a good relationship with them. They can discuss your plans with you before you submit them for approval; they won't tell you for sure whether or not your proposal will be approved, but they may tell you if there are reasons why it won't be approved. They will also be able to tell you about any easements, covenants and overlays that might apply to the property. This is vital information if you are developing or subdividing.

➤ *Town planning consultant.* If you would like help with a council submission and management of surveyors, engineers and so on, you may want a town planning consultant. A good consultant will make sure your application conforms to council rules, and will manage the process for you so it doesn't take up as much of your time. A town planning consultant is also paid to be on your side, whereas a council town planner is paid to serve the council.

➤ *Land surveyors.* A land surveyor will measure the dimensions and slope of a property, confirm boundaries, locate services and prepare a report on the property, including a plan of a proposed subdivision which can be submitted to the planning authorities.

➤ *Builders, carpenters, plumbers and electricians.* Unless you are qualified to do any of this work yourself, you'll have to get people in to help in these areas. Good tradies will provide advice about the project, turn up when they are supposed to and get the job finished on time.

➤ *Building inspectors.* A building inspector will inspect the structure of an existing dwelling, looking for structural problems and compliance issues. They will be able to provide recommendations for how to rectify any problems found if you ask.

➤ *Draftsperson or architect.* If you are planning a development or subdivision, you may need one or both of these. An architect will cost more, but can come up with a creative and unique design for your property. A draftsperson usually has a technical background, and could come up with a more basic design that will be cheaper to build.

➤ *Engineers.* If your project involves moving power or water supplies, stormwater drains or sewerage, you may need an engineer. Your surveyor or town planning consultant should be able to tell you whether your project requires such work and, if so, engineering specifications will be required with your permit application.

➤ *Real estate agents.* Agents not only buy and sell your properties, they are a great source of information and can find deals for you. Get to know a few in each area that you invest in, and stay in touch with them regularly. Once they know you are serious and ready to buy they will be very helpful.

➤ *Solicitors.* There is a lot of paperwork involved in buying and selling property, and getting it all right is crucial. Your solicitor will be able to review all the paperwork involved in a deal—including title documentation, sales contracts and council applications — to make sure everything is being done legally and that you are getting the deal you have verbally agreed to.

➤ *Conveyancers.* A conveyancer's job is to manage the sales contract process for you. Keep in mind that a conveyancer is not a lawyer; if everything goes smoothly with your deal a conveyancer is fine, but if you run into problems you will need a solicitor. If you prefer to use a conveyancer, find one who has a relationship with a solicitor so that you can get help at short notice. If your deal is complicated, it might be best to use a solicitor from the beginning.

➤ *Lenders.* You have to get money from somewhere! Most people don't have enough cash lying around to buy a property outright. If you develop a relationship with your lender, you are likely to get better service, lower interest rates and more assistance if you run into problems. Mortgage brokers are a great place to start.

➤ *Accountants.* Seek advice from your accountant about the tax implications of your potential deal and the ownership structure that would best suit you and your deal. Make sure you do this before you sign anything, as changing the ownership structure later will likely be an expensive exercise.

➤ *Mentor.* Throughout the book you'll have read that the real deal investors all had mentors. The support of having someone who has been there before and is on your side adds a confidence to your decision making crucial for taking action, especially in the early days.

Many of the people we've heard from in this book have mentioned how important their team has been to their success. Have you started building your team yet?

> **On the road to financial freedom...**
>
> Get help from people who are familiar with the local area and know the requirements of the relevant planning scheme. Every area is different, so local knowledge is a great asset.

🏠 🏠 🏠

Steve and Mandy came to property after taking a hammering in the sharemarket. In just a few years they will have recovered their losses through property investing.

Notice how Mandy writes about her property investing. Her experience shows in the language she uses when she describes her deal. She didn't start out like this. Don't expect to have Mandy's level of experience when you make your first deal, but keep going. You will get there too.

Real deal: our three-block deal

Hi, my name is Mandy. My husband Steve and I are in our early 40s, and we are both very keen property investors. We live in Adelaide and have a young son.

Steve and I had a vision of what we wanted our life to be like, but at first we weren't sure how to get there. We both started off doing the 9 to 5 thing, but quickly realised we weren't going to reach our goals that way. In our jobs the income potential was limited and there was little flexibility. But now, thanks to investing in property, we are well on our way to living our dream. We've left the 9 to 5 world behind and are now highly dedicated to our investing. We haven't achieved financial freedom yet—but we have a target date! Now that we are investing in property we are much happier with our lives. We are earning more money than we ever thought possible, and this is allowing us to spend more time with our son.

Steve and I wanted to create wealth for ourselves for a number of reasons. Our ultimate goal is to be able to choose what we do with our time, what we spend our money on, and what we want to experience with our friends, family and community. We want our son to have a great life and not miss out on anything. Another goal of ours is to help disadvantaged people.

Time for an adventure!

After achieving his Bachelor of Business, Steve started out as a purchasing officer at a stationery company, then moved on to services manager at the SA Real Estate Institute. I started my career as a dental nurse, then became a dental therapist. We were both earning around $60000 per year. We both thought our jobs were okay, but we were also both restless and thought we could be doing something a bit more interesting or adventurous with our lives.

One day we came across a jet ski hire business for sale on the Maroochy River on the Sunshine Coast. Within three months of seeing that advertisement, we had sold our house and bought the jet ski business. Some of our friends and family thought we were crazy, but most of them also admired us for having a go and taking a chance.

We had an absolute ball working on the river. But again, after five years of this we were starting to feel that it was time for a change. We returned to Adelaide, where we helped Steve's parents with the running of their bed and breakfast business (five secluded, self-contained cottages on 200 acres, 30 minutes from Adelaide. Gorgeous!). Steve's parents retired in 2000 and we took over the reins.

The B&B business required our constant attention and the hours could be long. Despite reaching great levels of success, the B&B still presented us with a high-input business, and we soon realised that when 100 per cent occupancy was reached, there was no room or opportunity for expansion. As with many businesses, no matter how hard we worked there was a ceiling on what we could achieve. We became hungry to make a better future for ourselves.

Property or shares?

We knew that the two most common forms of investment are property and shares. We did have some experience with property. In 1998 we bought two units on one title, and were able to subdivide and sell them off individually. We doubled our money in five years, selling both, and paid off our own home. That deal was great for us. We really should have taken more notice of just how brilliantly real estate could perform for us, but instead we went in a different direction.

We tried the sharemarket, but we borrowed (in hindsight) too heavily, and got whipped as the market tumbled during the global financial crisis. We reached crisis point after receiving four margin calls, and sold the entire portfolio. We lost about $350 000! We had lost basically all we had worked for over the previous 10 years. It was devastating to experience such a setback, and almost overnight we felt like our goals had disappeared from view.

We should have tried property first...

Determined to get back on track, the next obvious option was to try property investing. Steve's family has a real estate background in every generation, back as far as his great grandfather. A number of Steve's family have been in sales, conveyance services and developing in all manner of strategies. We should have known, I guess. Steve's previous job was in the real estate industry. If you've done okay in property, you should stick with what you know.

Our three-block renovate and subdivide deal

In our first deal we were able to generate a $260000 profit by subdividing into three blocks, renovating and selling a 3000-square-metre property, one with a renovated home and two vacant battleaxe blocks behind the house. We came across this deal the day it was advertised in the paper and on the web. With our previous experience, we had the confidence to give this one a try.

We were attracted to this deal because a three-block subdivision gave more scope for profit than a two-block subdivision. We felt that selling off the new blocks as vacant land would be a profitable strategy for the area. We could have built houses on the blocks, but it wouldn't have been profitable for us to do this as the price ceiling for the area wouldn't have recouped the cost of the land and the cost of the house. Blocks were scarce in this area!

This deal turned out very well for us, and we think that subdivide, renovate and sell is a great strategy for making lump-sum gains.

On the road to financial freedom...

As a general rule, the more lots you can subdivide into the greater the profit. There will, however, be planning restrictions on how many lots you can create. And people don't want to live like sardines, so don't get carried away.

One of the first things we do with any deal is work out our borrowing capacity. We have a few lines of credit (a loan facility to access the equity in your house—speak to your mortgage broker) in place against our own home and another buy and hold property we own in conjunction with Steve's parents. Our B&B business enables reasonable cash flow that will also cover the interest on all the lines of credit, so the bank has been quite favourable to our requests. We approached the bank to let us know how much we could borrow, so were guided by their advice. We have made sure 20 per cent of the purchase price plus costs comes from our lines of credit at the moment, but as we complete more deals our plan is not to use these borrowed funds to save on interest.

Meeting the neighbours

One of the first tasks we tackled was to remove four insignificant gum trees that were encroaching on the anticipated building envelopes on our two new blocks, leaving 30-something remaining. At about lunchtime that day, Steve received a hostile visit from our neighbour who accused us of ruining the bird habitat (she obviously didn't see the natives we had just planted out the front of the house which would attract many birds!). We love birds around our own home so wanted to duplicate some of our 'bird-friendly' garden at this new home as part of the reno. That was awkward moment number one...

Then a planner from the council turned up wanting to see what was happening! Awkward moment number two. He didn't have a problem with what we were doing—we were operating by the book. But the neighbour was still emotional! We commented—with tongue in cheek—that if our neighbour was so worried about the birds being disrupted, maybe she should be doing something about her two large dogs that barked pretty much all day long. Maybe the birds would return around her place if the dogs didn't scare them away! It wasn't a friendly start to the project.

The next day Steve noticed that these neighbours had a couple of old trees that had dead limbs broken off and it looked very messy. He took a deep breath and offered to clean the branches up for them and clear the old wood around their yard. The response was favourable and so Steve started work. During all this, the husband came out and started asking Steve his thoughts on the chances of them subdividing their own block to build a house for their daughter. The area that he showed Steve was littered with trees, so we had a laugh about whether or not his wife would be prepared to cut down all those trees to enable them to build a home for their daughter. Apparently the development application has now been submitted to council!

An expensive mistake!

One small detail that we overlooked in our due diligence was whether or not the sewer ran across the front of the block along the road as it did in practically the rest of the entire road on both sides. As it turned out, in that small portion of the road the sewer actually stopped just before our place and commenced at the rear of the block next door, down on the rear boundary of the remaining houses. Our assumption that the sewer just continued along the same path was wrong. Once we had recognised this, we consulted with SA Water, paid them another $30 000 (yikes!) and had to stop traffic along the road for a couple of days while a trench was dug 50 metres further along, to enable our hammerhead block on the opposite side to have sewer connection. Ouch!

Ultimately it didn't matter. If we had known about this cost prior to commencement, we still would have gone ahead as there was still good money to be made in the deal.

On the road to financial freedom...

Never assume anything. Do your research and due diligence on every aspect of a deal.

Finding who our target market would be was just a matter of looking at area statistics and profiles of who was living in the existing homes in the area. As we lived in the same area, we had a good idea of who that might be anyway but it was still great to look at the statistics, which were readily available to us from the council website. Our target market was families, so we designed the house renovations so that a family could comfortably live in the home. We removed three walls to open up a large living space at the rear of the house, and put in French doors and window panels leading to an outside courtyard. We replaced the old kitchen and gave it a really light, airy feel, staging it then in a minimal contemporary style, which we knew would appeal to our market.

Time to sell

Steve's brother is the local real estate agent, and he designed a campaign for us that hit the market with a bang. The house had wonderful street appeal, and he anticipated great interest as blocks in this area are quite scarce, and fortunately for us there were no other properties in that township for sale when ours hit the market.

We were getting a number of hits on their website as well as <www.property.com.au>, and as we had one offer on the table prior to our first 'open for inspection' the structure of the sale then turned to putting in best and final offers. We had seven written offers after that first open inspection, and instead of receiving $395 000, which we went to the market with, we received $442 000!

This deal worked out so much better than we had planned. At the time we weren't factoring in any capital growth, but the area actually had grown in value, and from the early stages of our due diligence to the time we released everything on the market, prices had risen.

Our two vacant blocks, which were subdivided, sold for $235 000 each rather than the $210 000 that we had expected. As for the house, we were originally told to expect about $290 000, but we really hadn't communicated to Steve's brother just what we were planning to do to the place, so when everything was done he and his colleague agreed on putting it on the market at $395 000! Our renovations had certainly added a lot of perceived value, which was wonderful. Staging the property too, we believe, brought us in another $40 000.

We have all our own furniture now, and I have also now walked into an unexpected opportunity of staging a few properties for Steve's brother when he has a vacant house to sell. Great extra income while our furniture is not in use for our own properties, and this shows you the sorts of unexpected opportunities that can arise once you get out there and start taking action.

The figures

Our figures for this deal are shown in table 11.1.

Table 11.1: real deal figures

	Planned figures	Actual figures
Purchase price	$450 000	$450 000
Closing costs	$23 000	$23 000
Time period for project	12 months	11 months
Holding costs	$27 000	$27 000
Renovation costs	$30 000	$60 000
Subdivision costs	$30 000	$63 000
Selling costs	$15 000	$29 000
Sale price		
vacant blocks (total)	$420 000	$470 000
house	$290 000	$442 000
Profit	**$135 000**	**$260 000**

Not bad!

Before and after

Figure 11.1 shows some pictures that show some of the work that was done. It's remarkable what you can do to fix up a property.

Figure 11.1: the property before and after

Before	After

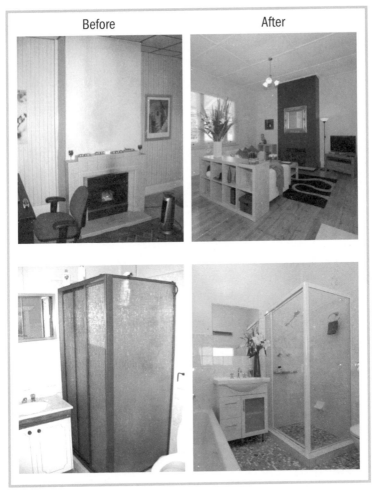

Before photos © Steve Adcock; after photos © Rob Scott.

On the road to financial freedom...

Referrals are a great way to find good, reliable people to add to your team. Talk to other investors about who they use, and when you hear about somebody who might be good, chase them up.

Our property team

Having a good property investing team allows Steve and me to spend time managing the operation and searching for new deals, rather than getting our hands dirty. Our team includes:

➤ a real estate agent, who also happens to be my brother-in-law.

➤ an accountant. Ours is also a property developer himself, so he really knows the ropes when it comes to real estate. He's been great.

➤ a conveyancer and surveyor. They are an essential part of our team.

➤ plumbers, electricians and builders. Knowing tradies personally creates accountability, which in turn creates great productivity.

We stay in regular contact with all of these people in the lead-up to and during a deal. Our next deal is going to be a complicated one, so we've also enlisted the services of a town planner.

On the road to financial freedom...

Only licensed plumbers and electricians are allowed to do plumbing and electrical work, respectively, so make sure you are hiring appropriately qualified people. Don't allow your builder or handyman to take on such work. And don't try to do it yourself!

Tips for new investors

We've learned some valuable lessons so far from our property investing. So that you can learn from our experiences, here are some tips to help you with your own investing:

➤ *Make sure you consult the council and look at the development plan before an offer is made on the property.* We feel this is so important to get a feel for what the council thinks about our plans *before* we place an offer on the property. We discuss our thoughts, and although they can't offer any certainty at that point you can benefit from a chat with them. Our local council is a wonderful source of information. For this deal we printed out the entire development plan from a link on the council website, and read through it with a fine tooth comb, so that we were totally familiar with the framework which enables development, and to also become aware of unique restrictions in the area that we might face. We tend to visit the development officers a few times during our due diligence phase to get a feel of what they are thinking. We have found that if you show that you are doing your best to help the council help you, they are more than happy to assist. We have found so much support from the council for our requests, but then we work hard at making those requests within the boundaries of the development plan structure. We try to give them no reasons to say no!

➤ *Take on board the services of land surveyors or other professionals.* We have found that employing the services of a land surveyor has been invaluable, as they have been able to see the possibilities of land subdivision from an experienced perspective, compared with our 'apprentice' view (though we are getting better as we go). Our experience tells us that our expected profit can increase dramatically simply by paying someone for their view of the best case scenario for the land. They usually have good contacts in council too, and will liaise with them on your behalf while you are establishing your own contacts at council.

➤ *Get hold of as much capital as you can, and also set yourself up with the best leverage scenario you can.* This will enable you to launch your investing momentum so much faster! Be disciplined and you will benefit!

➤ *Get out there and do lots of research first up.* When you begin, don't just expect to be able to look in a real estate agent's shop window and be able to discern what is a good deal or not. Lots of research and number crunching needs to happen before you can make an informed decision. Different areas perform well with different strategies, and it is so important to match the area with the best working scenario for that particular area. Getting out of the house and becoming an area expert is critical to your success.

On the road to financial freedom ...

Some accountants and lawyers specialise in small business, some in shares, some in property. Find a lawyer and accountant who have lots of experience in property.

My current situation

We are currently working on a two-block subdivision, renovation and sell, and by the end of the year will be working on a seven-block subdivision with two houses to renovate. We will be able to recoup our sharemarket losses in just two years, which we think is amazing! We would never have dreamt that we would be able to get back on track so quickly. Our investing is starting to change things for us in an incredibly positive way.

We now have five staff who keep the B&B wheels turning, so that we can put most of our efforts into real estate. At the moment it is still very worthwhile keeping our business going as the banks take into consideration our income from the B&B

for us to be able to borrow the funds needed for our investing. For this reason we'll possibly have this business running for quite a while, with minimal input from the two of us. We really now just oversee the business, by checking on things at the end of each month.

Our lifestyle is now one of flexibility and choices. Yes, there are businesses to monitor and a three-year-old boy to bring up, but already having generated extra capital has put us in a situation where our lines of credit are paid off and we are cashed up ready for our next project. It is becoming such an exciting time for us. We are now in our early 40s and it's time to make hay while the sun shines. All the opportunities we ever wanted are on our doorstep now, and having a means that actually works for us has lifted our spirits remarkably by giving us an assurance like no other that we can have a fantastic and comfortable future.

Looking to the future

Our aim now is to continue seeking out properties that are suitable for subdivision, with a dwelling in need of cosmetic renovation. We have found that this strategy works well for us, so we are sticking to what works for now. We want to switch to commercial property down the track as this better suits our aim of achieving passive income, and we believe that the percentage return on investment is greater than residential property with fewer hassles.

We anticipate achieving financial freedom when we own enough commercial property to earn us $200 000 passive income per year. This will be by 30 June 2018! We are confident of achieving this given the start we have had, and we are certain that we would not be able to achieve this without investing in property. Our property journey has given us our time and our life back and allowed us to chase our dreams. Of course we've hit some snags along the way, but we thoroughly enjoy what we are doing and get closer to achieving our dreams every day. Financial freedom for us means having freedom and choice. We believe if we work the right strategy now we will thank ourselves in the future!

🛒 🛒 🛒

Another great deal! Mandy and Steve have a target date for achieving financial freedom and are working hard to reach it. Do *you* have a target date for financial freedom?

Do something!

Read through this chapter and make a list of all the members of an expert property team. Next to each line write the name of the person in your team. If there are any blanks, now is the time to consider if you will need this expertise in your next deal. If so, it's time to make some phone calls.

Bonus content

To hear Mandy speak about her deal in more detail, go to <www.resultsmentoring.com/book1/>.

Part IV

Construction

Chapter 12

Construction

Construction for profit requires attention to detail, good project management skills and good people skills. Does this sound like you? Even a small project is a large undertaking, and more work is usually required than for any of the other strategies we have looked at so far. As a first-time add-value investor, construction of a dwelling might not be for you, but once you have one or two deals under your belt you might want to give one a try. There is great potential for profit in building, as you will see in Adam's deal.

Hands on, lump-sum cash/equity

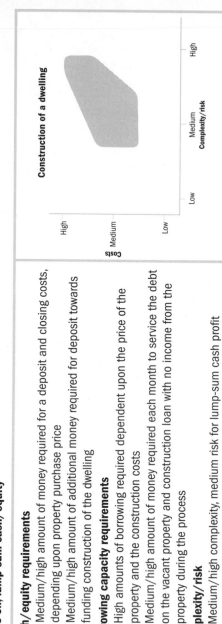

Construction of a dwelling

Costs: High / Medium / Low

Complexity/risk: Low / Medium / High

Cash/equity requirements

- Medium/high amount of money required for a deposit and closing costs, depending upon property purchase price
- Medium/high amount of additional money required for deposit towards funding construction of the dwelling

Borrowing capacity requirements

- High amounts of borrowing required dependent upon the price of the property and the construction costs
- Medium/high amount of money required each month to service the debt on the vacant property and construction loan with no income from the property during the process

Complexity/risk

- Medium/high complexity, medium risk for lump-sum cash profit

Skills requirements

- Medium levels of researching, area and deal analysis and negotiation skills will be required
- Medium/high levels of project management and people skills will be required

Time requirements

- Medium time will be needed to find, analyse, negotiate and buy property
- Low/medium time will be required to execute the construction as most of the day-to-day work is done by builder

Desired outcome

- Cash lump-sum profit or equity gain

Common mistakes

Not all deals go smoothly: despite hard work and the best intentions you can still make mistakes, and sometimes they can be costly. And developing a property is complicated, so there is lots of room for mistakes! Let's have look at some common errors and how you can avoid them.

Underestimating the complexity of the process

In construction or development, deals can be extremely complex and involved, particularly in larger multi-dwelling deals. There is a lot of research to do, a lot of decisions to be made and many different people to manage. If you don't perform your due diligence in sufficient detail or lose control of the project once it's underway you may experience significant financial losses.

To avoid these, do thorough research before you take the deal on. And then once you have signed the sales contract, create a plan for your project that takes into account all aspects of the construction or development. It's up to you to monitor the plan regularly as the project progresses, and if you start to see some deviations find out what the issue is and address it immediately.

On the road to financial freedom ...

Continually compare what you planned to do with what is actually happening. If there are discrepancies, find out why and address the problem immediately.

Losing control of the project

While you will have to employ numerous people to help you with your project, ultimately you are responsible for its success. You must manage the project closely and carefully, staying in regular contact with all members of your team and visiting the site to keep an eye on progress. You must manage your team, the money and the schedule to make sure your project is finished on time and on budget. You can start looking for your next project while your development is underway, but don't become too distracted by your next deal and forget about your current one.

Problems may arise at different times during your deal (just read about what happened with Adam and his tree!). When this happens, stay in control and consult your experts and ask them to help you find a solution. That's what you are paying them for!

Incorrectly estimating the end sale price

As you have seen throughout this book, accurately calculating your figures is essential to the success of any deal. Most of the expenses in a development or construction deal can be accurately estimated, but as with all deals it is impossible to be completely certain about your end sale price. This is one of the most important figures in your deal but the most difficult to be certain about.

The end sales price is a vital figure in your calculations. It is a critical number because the key to determining your purchase price for a property is to work backwards from your expected sales price. The idea is to do your due diligence to come up with an accurate end value for your deal, and then subtract the costs of developing, holding and selling to determine the maximum price you can purchase at to make an acceptable profit.

There are many different ways you can research sales prices, including:

➤ talking to real estate agents in the area

➤ purchasing one or more reports on the recent sales history in the area (for example, from RPData or Australian Property Monitors)

> ➤ using newspapers and the internet to study recent sales and houses currently on the market

> ➤ attending auctions or monitoring auction results to see what similar properties are selling for today.

You also can't simply forget about your end sales price once the project is underway. The market can change during your deal; this is especially true for developments because the time frame can be 12 months or more. Repeat your research into sales prices at regular intervals during the project, to make sure your figures are still relevant. Prices can move 5 per cent, 10 per cent or 15 per cent in 12 months (up or down). If they move in your favour, then great! If it goes the other way it could spell trouble for your deal, and you must sit down immediately and make some decisions about how to proceed.

Oversupplying the market

When you are deciding what type of development to do, keep in mind the laws of supply and demand. Are you planning on building units in an area already saturated with them? Are you building townhouses right next to a new estate? You can't simply build a dwelling and expect that people will buy it. It has to be the type of property that people want in that area, and there also has to be buyers for it.

Drive around the area and study real estate listings to see what's currently for sale. Are there lots of properties like yours on the market? If so, perhaps you need to come up with another plan, otherwise you might just be adding another unsold property to the market. If this happens you will either have to dramatically reduce your price or wait a long time to sell, neither of which will be good for the profitability of your deal.

> **On the road to financial freedom...**
>
> If what you are building is scarce and desirable in the market, you will have a much better outcome. Note that scarce doesn't mean weird or unique; in an area with lots of three-bedroom houses, a standard four-bedroom house will be scarce.

Ignoring the target market

You must know what your target market wants, including the benefits and features they are after and how much they will be willing to pay. If you build the wrong type of dwelling in the wrong area, it doesn't matter how nice it is, people won't be interested.

Be careful not to overcapitalise on your deal; that is, don't spend money on the property that will not help to increase your profit. For example, if you are building in a low income area, adding a room with a home theatre system won't necessarily bring you any extra profit because buyers may not be prepared to pay extra for something they don't really need. Buyers in this market are looking for affordability, and paying for an extra room with a home theatre won't be seen as good value. However, if you are developing in a high-income area the home theatre might help add to your profit because these buyers may be willing and able to pay extra for it; they may see it as a desirable feature rather than an unnecessary cost.

> **On the road to financial freedom**
>
> 'Build it and they will come' may have worked for Kevin Costner in *Field of Dreams* but it is an often fatal approach for developers. Build something because there is demand for it, not because you can.

Failing to budget for all building costs

Some novice investors fail to take into account all the costs involved in a construction project. You must scrutinise all builders' quotes carefully and establish what is and is not included, so that you are not surprised by any last-minute expenses.

Your budget should cover everything necessary to hand the property over to a buyer, including:

> construction costs

> service connections

> internal fixtures

> appliances

> floor coverings

> garage

> driveways

> fences

> landscaping.

Be aware that some aspects of a builder's quote could be subject to change. For example, the price for laying the foundation of the building could be subject to the quality of the soil. Different soil types require different construction methods, and if the soil quality is found to be low once building starts your costs could increase dramatically.

Make sure you have a detailed understanding of your agreement with the builder and what they will actually be delivering.

Failing to check access to services

Not every site is suitable for development or construction. Some sites require significant—and expensive—work to connect power, water and electricity. Check access to all services as part of your due diligence before signing anything. (Think about

Mandy's deal in the previous chapter. She didn't check the sewerage access to her property; she just assumed that it ran in front of the block but it didn't. Overlooking this in her due diligence cost her $30 000!)

Treating the council/planning authority as the enemy

While investors sometimes find dealing with councils and local authorities frustrating, it is important to keep them on side and well informed about your project if you want things to go smoothly. Get the council/planning authorities involved right from the planning stage of your deal. This will help you establish a relationship and find out early about any problems you might face. Be cooperative, and only put up a fight when you think you have been treated unfairly.

On the road to financial freedom ...

Try to find one or two people in the council/planning authority who you can develop a relationship with. Stay in regular contact with them and keep them informed of any changes in your project. This will help things go smoothly.

Managing cash flow poorly

Having good cash flow is critical for the success of your deal. There are consultants, builders, electricians, plumbers and so on to pay along the way, and you should also have some cash set aside for unforseen problems. You must carefully monitor all money coming in and going out, and continually study your budget to make sure you are on track. And stay in regular contact with your lender so there are no surprises for you or them. Many projects have gone bust because the developer didn't have enough cash to keep the project afloat during the building stage despite the profitability of the deal.

On the road to financial freedom...

When subdividing or developing a block the slope of the land is a very important factor. It is much easier to develop land that is flat or slopes gently towards the road.

Specifically for large-scale developing

Construction is a part of every development, whether it be building one, two or many dwellings on a block of land. In this chapter we introduce the idea of construction in its simplest form: buy a block of land and plonk a house on it. The points raised previously are relevant for any form of construction—single or multiple dwelling—but the following two points relate to multiple dwellings only.

Overcrowding a site

It's often true that putting more dwellings on a site can result in more profit, but there is a limit! The dwellings must still be attractive and comfortable to live in. Nobody wants to look into their neighbour's bedroom while having their morning coffee. If you have a site that could comfortably fit five dwellings on it but you think you would make more profit cramming eight in, you might be in for a surprise! You'll make more profit on five dwellings that people actually want to live in than eight empty ones that you can't find buyers for.

Failing to leverage pre-sales

It is possible to make a sale before or during construction. This is done by presenting plans and illustrations of the finished property to buyers. Pre-sales allow you to go to the lender with a clear perspective on the completed unit values. This will allow the developer to borrow against the end sales value rather than just the cost of land and construction. Being able to borrow more will release the burden of funding the deal entirely on their own, meaning more freedom with cash flow management. This is also often called selling 'off the plan'. Note too that larger scale developments will almost certainly require some level of pre-sales before the bank will lend for construction.

The possible downside of pre-sales is that sometimes buyers will expect to pay a lower price because they are unable to see the finished product. Think carefully about this and crunch your numbers: freer cash flow now might be better than holding out in the hope of a larger profit later. Take note of the outlook for the market. How confident are you of achieving a higher price when the project is complete?

On the road to financial freedom ...

Pre-sales will make your lender happy as it shows there is interest in your property at the right price.

🏠 🏠 🏠

Construction deals usually involve adding hundreds of thousands of dollars to a property, and this is not something you want to undertake lightly. It requires diligent project management from beginning to end.

Typically, construction projects fail in three areas:

1   investors underestimate costs

2   they take too long to complete the project

3   they fail to manage the cash flow.

Either of the first two outcomes will affect your profit. The lack of cash flow will stop your deal dead. It is critical that you prepare a detailed budget for expenses and a detailed schedule for time and cash management throughout the project. If you see any variation on the plan you need to modify future tasks to accommodate these changes so that you don't blow the budget in either time or money and your profits are preserved.

Adam is going to share his construction deal with us. Take note of how he managed his budget and schedule. And also how he handled a great big tree getting in his way!

Real deal: a successful plan B

Hi, my name is Adam. I'm in my mid 30s, married, with two lovely girls, one aged five months and the other five years. I recently worked with a large building company, but decided to go out on my own and fully explore the world of real estate investing, so I'm now a full-time property investor.

When I was a kid, my parents struggled at times to make ends meet, so from a young age I thought that I needed to do things differently so I didn't have the same fate. I didn't know much about shares, but some family friends whom I considered successful were involved in real estate investing. I guess that's how I was first exposed to property, and since then I've thought it could be a good option for me. My father also influenced me into property. He was a builder as well. And my mother has always supported and encouraged me. I bought my first property in 1998.

I'd read a few books and attended a few programs about real estate when I found the real estate program that I've now been involved with for about four years. I was a registered builder when I joined and had a couple of investment properties. After participating in the program, I began to realise how much more there is to investing and property. And I think I've learned just as much about myself and what I want in life as I have about property.

I was just looking...

I was browsing <www.realestate.com.au> and came across a deal in the eastern suburbs of Melbourne. It was a house in a nice leafy suburb in an old dilapidated state on 700 square metres. Initially I wasn't interested in buying it, but I do like to keep track of deals in the area, and I was curious to see what happened with it. (I keep a log of all relevant sales in the area.)

I had seen this site before and I thought it would be a good opportunity for someone to buy, knock down the existing house and build two townhouses. That's a strategy that I have been using and it's been working well. I know the area very well; I've learned that it's important to be an area expert. I had a good idea of what I would be able to buy it for, being in the industry I was confident of what I could build for, and knowing the area I was confident about what I could sell it for.

Still unsure on the day of the auction, I didn't go there to purchase, I was just driving past. I thought I would take a look just to see what was going on in the area. The house was so filthy inside that from the street you could almost smell it. There were quite a few people at the auction but I noticed that not many were bidding. I think most of the people at the auction just looked at the place as a dump and so didn't see the potential. The bidding was so low that I ended up buying it! And I hadn't even looked inside!

I knew the area and the numbers already, and so I knew what I was looking for. I knew that I needed to buy under $500 000 to make a deal work. If I could buy at this price and put a couple of new houses on the block I would have a good deal, so it didn't matter what type of house was on the property when I bought it as I was just going to knock it down anyway. So a smelly place that was about to fall down wasn't a problem — in fact it probably helped me secure the property at a good price.

On the road to financial freedom…

If you are well prepared and have done your planning and due diligence for the type of deal you are looking for, you will be able to make quick decisions about purchasing a property that fits your plan.

A hasty reassessment

I had already done due diligence on numerous similar properties in the area, and I had assumed that everything I had done could be applied to this property. But I thought it would be a good idea to double-check everything, so I did my due diligence again on this property. I had my draftsperson check on the overlays on the property: there was no vegetation overlay, heritage overlay or anything else that looked like it could be a problem — just as I had expected. So we went ahead and began to draw up the plans for the new houses to be built on the land. (An overlay is basically a restriction on what you can do with a property; for example, if there is vegetation on the property that you are not allowed to remove there will be a vegetation overlay.)

But when we went to our first council meeting, we found out that there was an 'interim' overlay on a 50-year-old, 20-metre Algerian oak tree that was registered as a Tree of Significance by the council. We found out that an 'interim' overlay does not come up when you do your title searches because an 'interim' overlay only means there might be an overlay in the future. I hadn't paid any attention to this tree as our searches told us there were no vegetation overlays on the property; now suddenly this tree was going to be a *big* problem. We needed to be able to remove it if we were going to complete the deal on the original plan.

My first thoughts were that this was an absolute disaster; my whole strategy had fallen apart. I had to decide whether to continue and contest the overlay, or change plans. I had some experts in to assess the situation, and was told that if I decided to contest the overlay it could go either way. We had no plan B at the time. I considered the options and calculated the costs involved. If we contested and won, it might cost $50 000 and we would lose a few months but we could still make $150 000. But if we contested and we lost, we would still lose $50 000 and a few months but then have to come up with a new plan anyway. It was too much of a risk, so we came up with a different strategy. We would drop the two townhouse development and build one house. At the time no homes in the area had sold for more that $950 000; this was a concern because when we did our new figures the total costs for a single home would be $1 million. But it was still the safer option given the circumstances. And the 'dying, ugly, dangerous' tree that should be cut down overnight turned into a healthy, beautiful oak that the home was designed around to maximise its wonderful presence (figure 12.3). When people started complimenting it nearing completion of construction, it had gone from ruining the deal to a selling feature of the home.

When I made the decision not to challenge the overlay, I thought I was going to end up with a smaller profit but this was the safer approach. In the end plan B gave me much more profit than expected with plan A, so not only was it the safer option it also turned out to be the most profitable.

On the road to financial freedom...

If you run into a significant problem with your deal, go back to the beginning with your figures. Crunch the numbers on different solutions to the problem and see what the best outcome is. As always, let the numbers decide.

Figure 12.1 shows the block being cleared (you can see the tree that caused all the problems) and figures 12.2 and 12.3 (overleaf) show the finished house.

Figure 12.1: clearing the block

Figure 12.2: the finished house

Photos © Alex Benci of Axiom Photography.

Figure 12.3: the tree became a feature of the property when it was finished

Photo © Alex Benci of Axiom Photography.

The figures

The approximate figures in the deal are shown in table 12.1.

Table 12.1: real deal figures

	Planned figures	Actual figures
Purchase price	$450 000	$450 000
Closing costs	$30 000	$30 000
Timeline	18 months	12 months
Holding costs	$45 000	$30 000
Construction costs (approx.)	$600 000	$500 000
Total costs	$1.1 million	$1 million
Sale price	Anticipated $650 000 for each house (we knew the area well so were confident of achieving this sale price). Expected sale value single house $1.1 to $1.2 million	$1.4 million
Profit	$200 000	$400 000

I sold at the end of 2009. I had the right property for the right buyer, and I found an agent who was getting good results with similar products in better areas. I don't think if I went with the townhouses that the deal would have been as successful. At the time I made this deal I was working 7 am to 7 pm in my job, so I made $400 000 in 12 months from what was basically a part-time job. You could say I'm very happy with the result! This outcome spurred me on to leave my job and attempt real estate investing full time.

Budgeting money and time

Even though I have created a budget, the profit will only be achieved if those numbers turn out to be accurate. I can estimate the sales price but can't be certain of this, as ultimately the market will decide for me. I know I can put a firm figure on the construction costs for a project, and from this I know I can determine my buy price. But none of this means anything if it's not done accurately, if I don't keep track of the figures throughout the project or if I don't stick to them.

The way I check that it's all going to plan is by breaking costs down into stages of development, so at each stage I can assess where I'm at. If I'm going over budget, I need to find ways to bring it back at the next stage. It is very easy to go over, and as I said the deal only works if I stick to the numbers. Change the numbers and my deal changes too. I think it's just like setting goals: it becomes very powerful when you write it down and consult it before making decisions.

It's also very important to create an accurate schedule for a project, and to stick to it. Going over time translates into more costs and reduced profitability for a project, so blowing my schedule also means blowing my budget. I usually allow 12 months for planning and approvals, and six to nine months for construction. As with my financial budget, I break my time budget down into stages (usually months), and work out what should be completed at the end of each stage. So, for example, at the end of the first month I might aim to have the base of a house completed, at the end of the second month I want the frame up, and at the end of the third month I want to be at lock-up stage (this means the walls, roof, windows and doors are in place and the house can be securely locked up). If you don't have a detailed schedule and budget in place before you begin, how are you going to monitor your project?

> **On the road to financial freedom ...**
>
> A blow-out in your schedule will most likely also mean a blow-out in your budget, through increased holding costs. Manage your time tightly!

My tips for other investors

From someone who is into construction, here are some tips that might help you:

➤ Engage a builder to manage the project for you. It will free up your time to look for other deals and focus on what is important. Our builder also managed the contractors/service providers for us.

➤ Challenging council rulings can be a time-consuming and expensive process. If you win you have still reduced your profit, and if you lose the results can be disastrous for your deal. So think carefully before challenging a council ruling, and explore all other options first. Sometimes it's better to cut your losses and move on.

➤ Become an area specialist, and find good deals by doing your due diligence and knowing your buying, building and selling prices.

➤ Educate yourself!

> Find a good builder you can trust and build a relationship with. Stick to someone who specialises in this area and someone you can deal with directly. This way you know you are playing with someone that has your project in his or her best interest. They are the business and they can be held accountable.

> Work out why you are doing all this and find your purpose. Ask yourself, 'If I do this deal and make this much, what will I do then? And then?' And so on until you work out what it is you really want. It will help you when times are tough and give you strength and purpose. Without it, you will have no fuel to drive your investing train.

My current situation

When I first started in property I worked from 7 am to 7 pm for a salary. I now work as a full-time developer/investor/builder, and I have created a plan to give me some balance in these three areas. I'm always learning and facing new challenges. I also ensure I have time with the family.

Looking to the future

I want to continue to build my team and I'd like to do a few more deals that are similar to this.

I've just bought my next project, a house on a large block of land. The plan is to move into this property with the family, and while we are living there to get the plans and permits underway to turn it into a two- or three-unit site. This is the first step. If it looks like a profitable deal, we'll then go ahead with the development.

My ultimate motivation is to create time for myself and achieve financial freedom. These two reasons are very powerful for me. I would like time for family, friends, and others who need help and guidance. Being financially free enables your mind and thoughts to focus on grander visions and actions to contribute to life rather than worrying and being anxious about surviving, paying the bills and mortgage. For me, real estate investing isn't just about property or numbers, it's about being able to enjoy a better life. I should be financially free by 40, but I will still continue to develop, invest and build because I love it!

🏠 🏠 🏠

This deal is a great example of how important it is to be ready for challenges and make informed decisions. Rather than letting his deal go off the rails when confronted with a problem, Adam consulted the experts, crunched his numbers again and made an informed decision. A very successful plan B.

Do something!

Consider your next deal in detail. Have you created a budget for the associated costs and expenses that might be incurred during this deal? If not, now is the time to list them. Become familiar with the cash flows for your next project and ensure you have the funds to be able to see the deal through.

Bonus content

To hear Adam speak about his deal in more detail, go to <www.resultsmentoring.com/book1/>.

Chapter 13

Developments

Now we are going to move on to residential developments. Developing is the ultimate form of 'adding value' through the construction of one or more new houses or units on a block. This is what Trevor did with great success, as you'll read about later in this chapter.

Developing sounds complex and difficult, but as you'll see from Trevor's deal it doesn't have to be.

What type of deal?

The first step in a development deal is to define the type of development you are going to undertake. There are several options available.

Hands on, lump-sum cash/equity

Development

(Chart: Costs (High / Medium / Low) versus Complexity/risk (Low / Medium / High))

Cash/equity requirements

- Typically medium/high cash requirements relative to other strategies
- Money required for a deposit and settlement costs, depending on property purchase price
- Money required for planning and consulting costs
- Money required for deposits for the construction of the dwellings
- Money required for finishing costs (carpets, landscaping and so on)
- High levels of money will be required each month to service the debt on the property and construction loan with no income from the property during construction

Borrowing capacity requirements

- High levels of borrowing will be required, dependent upon the price of the property and costs of construction

Complexity/risk

- High complexity, high risk for lump-sum cash profit

Skills requirements

- Medium/high levels of researching, area and deal analysis and negotiation skills will be required
- High levels of project management and people skills will be required
- Medium knowledge of construction process
- High levels of patience for dealing with planning authorities

Time requirements

- Medium amounts of time needed to find, analyse, negotiate and buy property
- Medium amounts of time required to engage and oversee consultants, builders and tradies, and for liaising with planning authorities

Desired outcome

- Lump-sum profit upon sale or equity gain

> *Single dwelling construction:* building on a vacant block, or taking a block with an existing house to be retained and adding another dwelling at the back or side.

> *Two-unit development:* dividing an individual lot into two separate lots and building two dwellings.

> *Multiple-unit development:* subdividing a property into three or more dwellings, potentially requiring common land to access the units.

> *Apartment houses:* creating a large block of units/apartments.

> *Housing estates:* larger sites with many houses built, usually on the fringe of existing suburbs.

As you are no doubt well aware of by now, you should choose your approach by evaluating your financial position, your existing skills, calculating the figures and seeing which strategy will best help you to achieve your goals. Start small and move up to larger and more complex deals as you gain experience, rather than trying to take on an office skyscraper as your first deal!

Planning for a development

Here are some issues that you must consider when planning for a development:

> *Target market.* Who do you think will purchase your finished 'product' from you? A homeowner? An investor? A family? A young couple? Retirees? Consider the needs of your target market before designing and building: their family situation, their age and income, the amenities they will expect and how much they will pay for a property. You can make a list of key features and benefits you think they will be looking for.

➤ *Target location.* Find an area where you see good potential for development, given your target market. Conduct research on the areas you are considering, so that you have a good basis for selecting a location. Find out who lives there now, and compare this with your target market.

➤ *Market research.* Find out how much your target market will be willing to pay for your finished product, and whether this fits with what you expect to sell for. You can talk to agents and study property data to get an idea of prices in the area.

➤ *Land prices.* You must research prices of available land in the area. This will help you determine whether a site you are looking at is good value. If a site you are looking at already has a building on it, this will also help you determine whether the property is being sold at 'land value' or at a premium for the existing building.

➤ *Finance.* Arrange your finance in advance, so that you are ready to respond quickly when you find a deal.

Once you have done your research on your market and identified where you plan to buy, you are ready to start targeting specific properties.

On the road to financial freedom...

Always overestimate the length of a deal. It's not uncommon for delays to occur and for developments to take 50 per cent longer than expected (or more).

Will your development be approved?

Once you have found a property that has potential for development you can contact the local council (or a central planning authority) to check that your proposed project would comply with all relevant regulations. Some of the issues you will need to address are:

➤ whether the zoning of the area permits what you are trying to do

➤ whether your development will meet all of the requirements around minimum lot sizes

➤ whether there are any overlays on the site that might restrict what you can do; for example, heritage, flood or vegetation overlays.

There are various authorities that will be involved in approving the proposed development. These include sewerage, water, gas, electricity and telephone authorities, and road authorities if your development requires road work. Making contact with each authority early in the process will help ensure you are aware of any issues or costs involved with compliance.

Inspecting the site

Check the physical conditions on the site, as these can help or hinder your development. Some features to carefully check include:

➤ existing crossovers (driveways), and the potential for adding more if needed

➤ any large or protected trees that could cause a problem (remember Adam's deal in chapter 12?)

➤ potential overshadowing or other issues that might upset the neighbours

➤ the slope of the land (it's more costly to build on a slope)

➤ the geology of the site—for example, is it rocky or sandy—as this can affect the costs of creating building foundations

> ➤ whether any prior use of the property could have contaminated the site; for example, fuel contamination from underground tanks at a petrol station

> ➤ any public assets that could interfere with the development, such as bus stops or power poles right where you'd like to put another driveway

> ➤ whether the site measurements match the details in the advert and contract of sale.

Now, we're not suggesting that you need to be a geologist or a town planning expert. Seek advice from a land surveyor or town planning consultant to get the answers you need.

You also need to obtain and review the property title, checking for any easements (such as sewer pipes crossing the property) or restrictive 'covenants' on the title that might prevent you from developing a block the way you want to.

If you've done all of the above and think that you might be onto a good deal, it's time to undertake a detailed feasibility study, analysing whether there is likely to be enough profit in the deal. If not, it's time to move on to the next deal.

On the road to financial freedom...

When conducting your due diligence on a deal, ask 'what if' questions to help find any problems. For example, 'What happens if the deal takes three months longer than expected?', 'What happens if prices turn down while we are working on the property?', or 'What happens if the council will only approve four units instead of the desired five on the site?'

A critical success factor in developing will be what you are able to sell the end product for. To increase the chances of achieving a good selling price it's a great idea to stage your properties for sale. Let's see how this is done.

Achieving a maximum sales price through staging

While there is often a requirement for at least some of the houses or units in a development project to be sold off the plan in order to get construction finance approval, there can be an advantage in reserving some of the sales until completion (as long as the cost of holding the dwellings for a time after construction is not an issue). This is because people will often pay more for a new home if they can actually see and inspect the building—it's not just a drawing on a piece of paper—and move in right away rather than having to wait several months for it to be finished.

You may not have heard the term 'staging'—it involves improving the presentation of the property for inspections, with the aim of achieving a higher selling price or selling more quickly. A well-presented home might sell for several thousand dollars more than you expect, but it might only cost you $1000 to stage.

Staging is more than just cleaning up and clearing the site once work is complete, or removing the pile of rubble. It's about creating an atmosphere in the house that is welcoming to buyers and helps them imagine living there. As you have probably noticed, many of the investors in this book have used property staging to increase their selling price and profit.

When staging, try to highlight the best features of the property. If it has a large lounge room, place a large lounge suite in there. If it has a great outdoor entertaining area, set up a barbecue and outdoor setting. If there's a great view, set the lounge suite up in front of the window. Wander around the house and think about how it will look to people who are seeing it for the first time. What attributes of the house can you highlight that will appeal to buyers?

Some ways to add to the appeal of a property include:

➤ If the house is empty when you are selling, hire some furniture. Put a couch and coffee table in the lounge room, beds in the bedrooms and a table in the dining room.

➤ Put some paintings or mirrors on the walls.

➤ Put some books and a lamp on a bookshelf.

➤ Place towels and fragrant soaps in the bathroom.

➤ Put flowers in the kitchen.

➤ Hire professional cleaners to make the property shine (including the windows).

➤ Consider the colour scheme of the house. For example, light, earthy tones are great.

➤ Tidy the gardens, mow the lawns and trim the bushes. Remove any rubbish, and if your car is an old bomb don't park it in the driveway.

When you are preparing the home for sale, remember that you are hoping to appeal to buyers, so don't prepare the home as though you were going to live there. Even if hot pink is your favourite colour, that doesn't make it a good colour for the towels in the bathroom. And *Star Wars* might be your favourite movie, but a nice Monet on the wall might be more welcoming than Darth Vader. Remove any family photos — remember, you want the buyer to imagine that they live there, not that they are adopting your kids.

Consider both the inside and outside of your property when staging. People form an impression of a property the second they pull up outside; if your property doesn't have 'kerb appeal', many potential buyers won't even make it inside. They probably have seven other places to look at that day, so why waste time on yours if it doesn't even look good from the outside?

So how do you decide where to start? Think of a potential purchaser coming to an open inspection. You have maybe 20 minutes to get them interested. The best way to do this is to appeal to the five senses:

➤ *Sight.* What visual features of the house will most appeal to your potential buyer? If you can see any, emphasise them! But if you can see any distracting features like cracks or awkward angles, then de-emphasise those.

➤ *Sound.* It's important that the house feels solid, and sounds are a big part of this. Creaky floorboards, squeaky cupboards and rattling windows do not convey a feeling of quality. These can be cheap and easy to fix, but will dramatically improve the feel of the house.

➤ *Smell.* Once again smells reflect the quality of the property. If the place smells dirty or musty, this is a big turn-off for buyers. Ensuring the place is squeaky clean will help with this. And some tried and true tricks include brewing some coffee before the inspection, baking some bread or burning a scented candle. People know about these tricks, but they still work. Also make sure the house has been aired out in the days leading up to the open inspection.

➤ *Touch.* This refers to how solid the place feels. If the door handles are loose, the cupboards stick and the floors are uneven, the overall impression of the property will be that the quality is poor.

➤ *Taste.* Unless you expect people to lick your wallpaper, taste refers to the ambiance of the house. For not too much expense you can create a consistent colour scheme and style throughout the house. Be tasteful!

Going to this effort will cost some money, but if you do it right it will more than pay for itself in an increased sales price or faster sale. If you have questionable taste (be honest!) or have no idea how to decorate a home, you can pay somebody to do the home staging for you. Simply do an internet search for 'home staging' to see the options. There are also many books available that can help.

The benefits of staging can include:

➤ a higher selling price

➤ a greater profit

➤ a quicker sale

➤ a better looking property for the marketing photos.

With every decision you make, keep in mind that you are not just trying to make the place look pretty, you are trying to increase your profit. Think about your buyers and what will attract them. Think about the type of house they will want to live in, and then do your best to create this environment. For a reasonable expense you can significantly increase your profit if you get the staging right.

🏠 🏠 🏠

Trevor may have his head in the clouds when it comes to his favourite recreational pastime — flying planes. However, when it comes to property investment he has his feet firmly planted on the ground. He lives by the ethos that 'your attitude controls your altitude!' In other words, if you truly strive to be successful, you can fly to the clouds and beyond.

Real deal: flying high

Hi, my name is Trevor. I'm 47 years old, and I live near the seaside about two hours from Melbourne with my beautiful wife. I'm a civil engineer, and at the moment I do my property investing in my spare my time.

Why I chose property

I spent my formative years living in rental accommodation with my mother and sister. My father passed away early in my life and my mother had the task of raising my sister and me. She worked exceptionally hard and provided us both with private educations, to her own detriment. As a consequence she had to rely on the government for support. Our humble flat, located in Melbourne's inner suburbs, was what initially inspired me to get into property. Well, actually my mother's landlord inspired me! Yes, it sounds weird, but I could see that mum's landlord was paying off his mortgage with her money and I thought that is what I should strive to do later on in life when I had the opportunity.

When I turned 18 I made the decision that I would never rent as I saw it as lining someone else's pockets. I made a decision early on not to be in a position where I would have to rely on the government to provide me with a pension later in life. Thanks to my property investing, I am now able to look after my mum and pay her back for the many things that she did for us when we were growing up.

I decided property was my best option when it came to wealth creation. My analytical instincts told me that housing has historically been a secure investment and therefore simpler to finance, with banks more than willing to lend money for property pursuits. Bricks and mortar have always been considered more secure for lending and as a result property allows a higher gearing ratio compared with other investment strategies. In other words, property allows me to leverage other people's money to a higher degree.

My first property

At 23 I bought my first property at the seaside location of Inverloch. We had been camping there for summer holidays for 14 years and a house that I had envied for ages came up on the market. I purchased this home for $61 500. I required a 20 per cent deposit plus costs to cover the bank's lending parameters, equating to around $14 000 of my own hard-earned cash. The house's current market value now sits at just under $700 000, having experienced growth that would make most residential property investors turn green with envy. Overall its market value has inflated by around 11 times its original purchase price in 1987, or at a staggering 11.5 per cent per annum. I've also added a number of other properties to my portfolio since this one.

Turning to development

In 2004 I decided as part of my financial strategy to become a property developer. In December 2003 I had realised the market was flattening out and I found it was getting harder to purchase blue-chip properties at the right price, so I thought I would create my own market by becoming a developer.

The aim was to buy at wholesale prices. I could see how this could be done developing the property myself, rather than buying some other developer's finished product. I would save on the developer's margin, GST, advertising costs, stamp duty and so on, meaning that the final cost of each completed townhouse could be $80 000 to $100 000 below its market value.

I started scouring the property market in November 2004 looking for a two- or three-townhouse site. I finally found two adjacent blocks in the inner-city suburb of Ashwood in March 2005 through a buyers' advocate, providing a total developable land area of 1600 square metres. Both blocks had an existing three-bedroom weatherboard house. Getting two blocks next to each other allowed me to get a fifth townhouse on the combined site and made the project much more profitable. The process of developing is the same for a two-house or five-house subdivision, but five will take a little longer to build and cost a little more.

A six-month settlement period was negotiated, which allowed me to get the development approval with only a 5 per cent deposit. The contract price for the two blocks with a house on each was $860 000. We obtained approval in July 2005, completed engineering drawings in August and signed the construction contract with a builder in October 2005. Construction began in November.

When I first began looking, my borrowing eligibility allowed me to develop a maximum of three units only. With the addition of two more dwellings to the project, along with the purchase of another piece of land, I took the opportunity to initiate a joint venture with two friends, as the bank required extra funds to get the project underway. I became the project manager, ensuring that the project ran smoothly, dealing with the town planner, administering the financials, negotiating finance and organising joint venture meetings. (Although the joint venture helped get the deal off the ground, it did cause problems later on when one of the joint venture members changed his investing strategy. We did of course have the agreement well documented, but things didn't go smoothly and the friendship was strained.)

On the road to financial freedom ...

Joint ventures and money partners can be a great way to take on deals that might otherwise be out of your reach, but there can be consequences if not all members have the same vision for the deal once it is underway. Relationships can be tested. Having your agreement well documented will help to prevent some issues and might help you to deal with problems if and when they arise. Before entering into any kind of joint venture or money partnership, always seek good professional legal advice.

I obtained three quotes for the construction. We asked three different builders to quote on a fixed price contract using a very detailed specification. This is extremely important; you must include every bathroom fixture, what colour everything will be painted, what materials will be used—every part of the construction must be covered down to the finest detail to ensure that you get the outcome you are after at the price you expect. As a consequence I receive very minimal cost variations to the fixed price contract, which the bank loves!

I managed the project myself—this is where I could bring my complementary engineering skills into the project. The project management included working with the town planner, local government, structural engineer, landscape designer and lawyers; reviewing plans; negotiating with lenders; arranging and assessing tenders; negotiating with the builder; preparation of contract documentation; assessing progress claims and issuing progress certificates; preparation of defects list; and engagement of a staging consultant and a real estate agent for selling.

As this was my first development project I also engaged an experienced project manager who dealt with the builder for me.

The project was completed at the end of August 2006, and it worked out as well as I had planned. It was completed on time and we got the prices we were looking for, and I think we produced a great product. As this was my first development deal I learnt absolutely heaps about real estate developing.

The images in figure 13.1 show different stages of the project, from demolition through to completion.

Figure 13.1: stages of the project

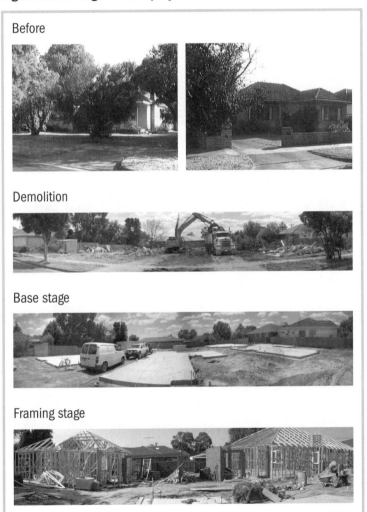

Figure 13.1 *(cont'd)*: stages of the project

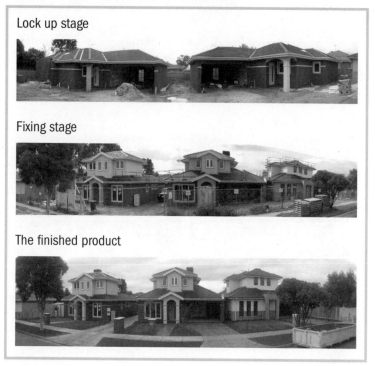

Lock up stage

Fixing stage

The finished product

Photos © Trevor Dando.

The figures

The figures for the deal are shown in table 13.1.

The 24 months of this deal included 12 months planning and 12 months construction. During the planning phase we rented out the two existing houses, which earned us some extra income.

We also added some extra profit by selling off one of the old houses rather than knocking it down. We found a company that will buy an old weatherboard house and remove it from the property, to later be re-sold. So rather than paying to have the house removed, we made some extra profit! And this also helps the environment because that house will be re-used. The other house was brick so it had to be knocked down.

Table 13.1: real deal figures

Expenses	
Purchase price	$860 000
Closing costs	$50 000
Time	24 months
Holding costs	$96 000
Construction costs*	$1 203 000
Selling costs	$11 500
Total expenses	*$2 220 500*
Income	
Sale price**	$2 443 500
GST input credits	$101 000
Rental income	$32 000
Total income	*$2 576 500*
Profit	**$356 000**

* Construction costs includes the cost of building plus all design and consultancy fees, including the town planner, architect, soil reports, civil engineering and structural engineering.

** Sale price also includes GST and the price for selling the removable home too.

On the road to financial freedom...

Always look for creative ways to save on costs and add extra profit.

We kept selling costs down by managing some of the sales ourselves. In hindsight this wasn't such a good idea. As a real estate agent, I'm a good civil engineer, so running a private sales campaign wasn't a good use of my time. Real estate agents are experts at selling property, so pay them to do what they do best!

Contingency planning

I always have a few contingency plans up my sleeve in case situations change. For this deal the first contingency was that we could have sold the blocks with planning permits if we thought that it was all too much to go through with the construction. Fortunately we decided to go ahead as there was much more profit available in the deal than just selling the endorsed town planning permits.

The second was that if we did not get our expected selling prices we could rent the houses out with a slightly negative cash flow. This is a benefit of developing yourself and essentially paying a 'wholesale' price for townhouses. If you were to buy the completed townhouses they would have been very negative cash flow.

On the road to financial freedom...

Have contingency plans so that if you run into a problem you can take action immediately. Don't just keep going in the hope that everything will work out somehow. Inaction doesn't usually solve a problem — it just makes it worse.

Managing service providers

To successfully manage all the different people in your project you must be very clear about the outcomes that you want and have this all well documented. It's also important to be proactive and plan ahead. I always try to think about eight weeks ahead, so that I can — hopefully — see what problems might be coming up.

It's also helpful to be a really good people person. I get on the phone and chat regularly to everybody in my team, and when problems arise I sort them out immediately. Procrastination just makes problems grow — they won't just go away if you bury your head in the sand. I think I'm good at managing people and this is one of the reasons I enjoy property investing.

My team doesn't just include tradies—I work closely with my lawyers, real estate agents and accountant as well.

> **On the road to financial freedom...**
>
> Conflicts can occur from time to time. The best way to deal with them is to try to create win–win outcomes for everybody involved.

My portfolio

I am definitely a long-term thinker when it comes to building my property portfolio. I rely on above-average rental yields to fund some of my positively geared investments and more up-market acquisitions to ensure respectable gains in the future. Although my residential portfolio is geared at close to 70 per cent, a diversification into shares reduces the overall gearing to a comfortable 65 per cent, which is where I like to remain. My rental yields vary from 3.6 per cent to 8.6 per cent; my blue-chip properties, which are creating my main capital growth, are yielding 3.9 per cent.

In terms of dollar income, the portfolio generates $230 000 per annum while my loan commitments total $300 000, making a shortfall each year of $70 000. I consider this a small price to pay for a capital gain of $450 000 per annum based on 7 per cent capital growth. In other words, I am coming out ahead $380 000 per year, which is not a bad salary to draw.

Until recently I was exclusively a Buy and Hold investor, having never parted with any of my properties for close to 20 years. However, times have changed and to leverage into larger development projects I sold a few of my properties in 2009 and 2010 to have cash available.

My methodical approach does not stop at the dollars and cents of a real estate transaction. I'm also very aware of market demand and providing a product that the renting public will want, so I stick to a housing configuration that I believe works. I always look at three- to four-bedroom residences, whether they be townhouses or houses. They give me more flexibility when tapping into the rental market.

Location, location, location

I focus my efforts in Victoria alone, having lived here all my life and feeling comfortable with the local real estate market.

I use the Australian Bureau of Statistics website to garner a thorough understanding of any area I am considering purchasing in. I think this is a critical step in the due diligence process. Some of the factors I look at are the number of owner-occupied versus rented properties in the area, the average number of occupants living in dwellings in the area and the age profiles of people in the area I am looking at developing or buying in.

My tips for new investors

My tips for new investors are:

➤ Educate yourself as much as possible, but don't do so much analysis that it causes paralysis.

➤ Research your market thoroughly.

➤ You make your money when you buy through having researched and thoroughly crunched the numbers and then managing the development process effectively, not when you sell.

➤ Find a mentor whom you are comfortable with to bounce ideas off.

➤ Surround yourself with trusted professional people as it is impossible to know everything related to all the disciplines required to grow and manage a substantial property portfolio.

> If you are switched on, apply yourself and stay focused with a goal in sight, then you will always reach it. Maybe not in the time frame you wanted, but you will reach it!

> An astute investor will always monitor the market and its particular cycles to determine what prices are doing; however, there are always 'once in a lifetime opportunities' out there. You just have to do the right research and look for them and make sure the numbers stack up.

> Attitude controls altitude.

My current situation

I love doing my engineering work so I will still work in that arena for another three years. I manage to fit my property investing into my spare time after work. I find the two actually complement each other. I am currently financially secure and have the opportunity to do many activities that I like, including a range of volunteer work, flying and travelling overseas.

Looking to the future

I have completed seven development deals to date, and my aim from now is to have four property development projects occurring each year. One of my criteria is to have a minimum profit of $150 000 per project.

Property investing, most recently property development, has given me a raft of options that I did not have when I commenced. It's given me the opportunity to have more than four weeks of holidays per year and to work part time if I choose to. I can provide for my mother, and it will also allow me to be a stay-at-home dad when children come along.

As for my long-term goals, I'm looking for a net income of $350 000 per annum from my investments. I will continue to be aggressive and grow the portfolio to $10 million and then reassess when I have reached this goal.

At 47 super for me is not an issue, so I only put the bare minimum into my fund as I can make a lot more return through property investing. I am intent on creating personal financial freedom to ensure a comfortable and fulfilling lifestyle when I quit my day job. At this stage I can't see that I will ever cease my property investing activities as I enjoy it so much. Later on I will be less aggressive in the growth of the portfolio and move into a consolidation phase.

By that time I will be 50 and it will be time to enjoy the benefits of all the hard work. At this point in time I will start to reduce the debt in the portfolio as I feel I will need more security for my family at that stage in my life.

🏠 🏠 🏠

Isn't Trevor inspiring! His success reflects everything we speak of in the book about research, due diligence, analysing numbers, financial awareness, having a strong *why*, choosing the right strategy for you, knowing the economy and being an area expert. He's got it down to a fine art, and as a result has been able to achieve his substantial portfolio for wealth part time. Congratulations Trevor!

Do something!

Find an area where you see good potential for development. Find out who lives there now, and think about who your target market would be. Look for examples of new housing, units and so on that have sold recently. What are people buying? What are they paying? And could you develop something similar for a profit?

Bonus content

To hear Trevor speak about his deal in more detail, go to
<www.resultsmentoring.com/book1/>.

Part V

Systemisation

Chapter 14

Developing a system

As this book has progressed we've looked at strategies that get more involved and more complex. The structure of the book follows the traditional path of a professional property investor as your skills, confidence and resources grow, leading to a marriage of your passions, belief and ability. This is the path to property investing success. Once you've had one or two successful deals, you may want to take your investing to the next level. This means turning your property investing into a repeatable system that you can apply over and over again to achieve greater profits with less effort.

But before systemisation can occur, you must become an expert in your strategy. Let's have a look at this.

From hands on to hands off, from cash to cash flow

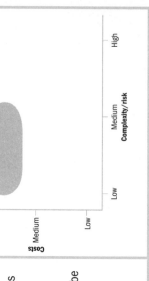

Developing a system

Cash/equity requirements

- High amount of money required for multiple deposits and closing costs, depending upon property purchase price and strategy employed as a system for generating wealth
- Money required each month to service the debts of multiple properties will depend on the strategy employed

Borrowing capacity requirements

- High amounts of borrowing are likely to be required, dependent upon the price bracket and number of properties held simultaneously. May be offset by any rental income from the properties.

Complexity/risk

- Medium complexity; risks associated with the system are offset by expertise in the chosen strategy

Skills requirements

- High levels of researching, area and deal analysis and negotiation skills will be required
- High levels of project management and people skills will be required
- Detailed knowledge of chosen strategy is essential

Time requirements

- Time will be required to focus on finding, analysing, negotiating and buying property
- Time will be required to engage and manage team to execute the strategy
- Reduced time requirements per deal, due to efficient outsourcing of day-to-day tasks

Desired outcome

- Financial freedom through both cash flow and accumulating assets

Being a strategy expert

As we mentioned earlier, there are two different ways you can approach your investing. You can focus on your strengths and outsource your weaknesses, or you can build up your skills in all aspects of investing and eliminate your weaknesses.

While eliminating your weaknesses may seem like a good idea, this approach can mean that you won't be an expert in any particular aspect of investing. If you spend all your time trying to master every aspect of investing, you won't have the time to become an expert at anything. You will be a generalist. As the saying goes, jack of all trades, master of none.

Building on your strengths will turn you into an expert, and this is what is required if you are going to have success with systemisation. For example, if you become an expert at reading trends in the market you can become an expert at short-term growth deals, and simply buy and sell over and over again. You will be able to pick pockets of growth and simply ride the increase in prices.

A strategy expert is somebody who knows:

> how the strategy works

> the outcome of the strategy

> the numbers of the strategy (this is vital)

> the time frames

> the people required to make the strategy work

> the specific terminology and language spoken by those involved with the strategy

> the areas where the strategy will produce the greatest profit.

If you don't understand any of these aspects of your strategy, you are not an expert. The system you create may be flawed and you might struggle to make it work. Ensure that you have completed a number of successful deals in the strategy you have chosen before attempting to create a system with that strategy.

Once you are a strategy expert, a whole new world will open up to you. Your belief in achieving financial freedom will be stronger than ever because you know what you are doing. Being an expert in your strategy will give you the ability to create your system. This will also allow you the confidence to let others do things on your behalf, which is an important part of building your team.

Creating a property investing system

Once you're an expert in your property investing strategy, the next step is to turn your strategy into a system that will dramatically reduce the amount of time required for your investing. You can think about creating your investing system when you have achieved the following:

➤ You have chosen a strategy based on your skills, financial situation, time requirements and desired outcome.

➤ You have created a description of your ideal property for your chosen strategy.

➤ You have become an expert in an area or a number of areas.

➤ You can accurately assess the potential return on a deal before you buy the property.

➤ You can consistently complete deals achieving the desired profit in the desired time frame.

➤ You have the financial resources to undertake more than one deal at a time.

This is clearly not a description of a novice investor. This is the stage wealthy and successful investors are at: after many years they know what works and what doesn't, and they have streamlined their processes so that they can achieve a great return by managing their system rather than individual deals.

On the road to financial freedom...

Experienced, successful investors are human too, and they were once investing rookies. When you start out, achieving this level of skill may seem like a dream, but with effort and perseverance you will get there.

So what does it actually mean to have an investing system?

Having an investing system means that you have built up a team of people and created processes that allow you to spend your time going out and finding deals, and then handballing the project to your team for them to do the work. For example, if subdivision is your chosen strategy and you have somebody whom you can rely on to manage the subdivision process for you, that's one less thing for you to do. If cosmetic reno is your thing and you have a group of tradies whom you trust to make the right decisions and complete the job, you can leave them to do the work. You must of course still be involved in the project and stay in touch with what is going on, but the day-to-day running and the nuts and bolts of the project are managed by your team.

The aim of creating a system is to free up your time. As a sophisticated professional property investor your main responsibility is to find the deals that make you the money you want. Once you have found them, you can then pass the project on to your team. This will give you more time to do the things you enjoy and are good at; something everyone wants from their investing.

Remember, every system is as individual as the investor, and a good business model keeps going while you are not there. A perfect system means that the process is even better when you get back from holidays than it was when you left. If you've made yourself almost superfluous, you've done it! Well done! Now you can spend your time doing what you want to do, and only minimal effort is required from you to oversee your investing system.

This is about making your active 'hands-on' projects operate as efficiently as possible. In the next chapter we'll look at the final step of turning your property empire into a 'hands-off' source of passive income.

On the road to financial freedom...

The role of the investor is to manage the overall system, rather than each step in the strategy.

Building the foundations for your system

With every property deal you undertake, you are learning and gaining experience, and also — hopefully — growing your capital base. These are the foundations of your investing system. If you are a renovator, each reno you do can teach you something. You might also add another member to your team, and discover a quicker way to fix up a kitchen. On your next deal you might find a new supplier who can meet all your hardware needs, saving you the hassle of dealing with a number of different suppliers. All of these add to the foundation of your system as your skill and experience grows, and you can take this into your future deals.

Throughout the book we have referred to financial freedom as a journey, and if you are at the point where you are ready to create a system you are nearing the end of this journey. You have reached this point by taking one step at a time, not attempting one giant leap. How do you know when you are at this point?

Let's go right back to the start of our journey. When you started out in property investing, perhaps you were only just making ends meet financially. This is why many people get into property. Living like this means that money drives all of your decisions. You often have to work hard just to pay the bills. You might want to go out for a nice dinner but can't afford to, so you drive past the nice restaurants and go to the fish and chip shop instead. You watch the football on TV rather than going to the game to save money. Money is affecting almost every decision you make.

When you start to have some success with your investing, money becomes less of a problem and a whole new perspective on life opens up to you. Going to a nice restaurant isn't an issue. Planning a weekend away isn't a problem. You can go to the footy every weekend, or to a movie, or to a concert. Going out isn't an escape or a treat any more, you do it just for the enjoyment and don't have to worry about the cost. This is the world you start to open up to yourself once you have some success with investing. It leads to a greater sense of awareness and purpose, and it becomes a given — rather than an ambition — that you will succeed. And the further you go, the more certainty you will feel.

As you gain experience, you will begin to develop your team as you work on different types of deals, find areas where you can make profitable deals, and know your own strengths and weaknesses. You can see opportunities that others can't because you know what is possible. You develop a level of confidence and understanding about your property investing and how to use it to create cash flow or lump-sum deals.

But ... you're not quite where you want to be yet. You can probably see it and taste it, but you haven't arrived at your destination yet.

By now you might be working part-time and doing your property investing a few days per week. Perhaps you are seeing that you are earning more — maybe much more — from your investing than your job. But maybe you can't find a way to focus exclusively on your investing. Deals, while successful, might be a little haphazard and based partly on your ability to find the time to do them.

The task now is to reflect on what you have done and build further on your strengths, and delegate those things that you aren't so good at or don't enjoy doing. You must refine the strategy that has given you the best results. It's time to map out on paper how you can plan to make one purchase and get the project underway, and then find and make the next deal, and the next, and so on.

Research–Purchase–Manage–Sell

This is done by creating a Research–Purchase–Manage–Sell system. This means you have processes for the Research phase, the Purchase phase, the Management phase and the Sell phase of a deal. Such a structure allows you to incorporate multiple deals into your system at once.

Let's see how this works.

You begin the process by searching for deals, and once you have found one that warrants further attention you research it more closely as we have done throughout the book. This is the Research phase of your system. If the deal stacks up, you purchase it — you guessed it, that's the Purchase phase. Then the property goes into the Management phase. This is where you delegate the management process (except for any parts that you may still want to have direct control over). You now no longer have to worry about the day-to-day tasks and instead can focus on managing the profitability of the deal and spend your time looking for other deals.

Now the advantages of this type of system start to emerge. While the first property is in the Management phase, you can go back to the Research phase and find the next deal because you are not spending too much time on the management of the first deal. Once again you go through the Purchase phase if the deal stacks up, and hand the deal on to your management team. And then once that deal has gone through the buy stage, you can start analysing the next one. And so on, and so on. Each deal will progress through the four phases.

This steady flow of deals will create a steady flow of profits. Rather than completing one deal, and then saying, 'Okay, what now?', there will be a steady stream of deals at different stages, and so there will always be a deal at or near completion and therefore there's always profit on the horizon.

Using such a system means that your investment ability is limited only by your financial resources. You can easily have two deals on the go at once, or maybe even more. Your skill is in finding and researching deals, in negotiating and buying the properties and applying your strategy. You will be more profitable if you spend your time doing these things and outsourcing the other parts of the investing process. It is a better use of your time to build a team and spend your time managing them rather than doing all of the work yourself.

On the road to financial freedom...

A good investment system allows you to leverage your time using your team. Rather than doing all of the work yourself, you engage others to take on some of it for you so that you are free to pursue the next deal.

If you can create a system for yourself you can step back from the process and give yourself some breathing space. You are now no longer creating the process, you are taking advantage of it. You might feel a weight come off your shoulders because you will free up your time and not have to worry about where the next dollar or the next deal will come from. Your confidence in your system might allow you to relax a bit.

As you will see later in the chapter, Troy H is evolving his system. He's not quite there yet, but he has identified what he is looking for, he knows what to do with it when he buys it, he knows where to get the money and he has a great team that can make things happen for him. So now he can just go out and find the deals and buy them, and handball them onto his team and go looking for the next one.

Creating a system might seem daunting if you are not quite at this stage yet, but don't worry—you will get there. All successful investors do. You will grow into this level of skill and understanding over time.

Start at the shallow end

When building your investing experience, we don't believe in a sink or swim approach; the most common outcome of this is sinking.

You might say, 'Hey, if development is the best way to make a large profit, why don't I just start off with these?' But development is more complicated than a renovation and subdivision, and a renovation and subdivision is more complicated than a positive cash flow buy and hold deal. If you start at the less complicated end of the spectrum, you can build your confidence and skills and learn how to make profitable deals without risking the farm. If you jump in head first at the deep end you will most likely make many mistakes, and because the deep end is also the expensive end these mistakes will be much more costly than a mistake made on a smaller deal. And if you don't think it's possible to wipe yourself out financially on a single deal, dive in over your head and see how you go. You might be in for a nasty surprise.

Having said that, it is important to stretch yourself in order to grow. Aim to go just beyond your depth so that you are challenged and make progress, but stay close enough to the edge so you can easily grab on if you run into trouble. This may mean starting on smaller, more manageable, lower cost deals, having the support of a mentor who has done it before, and progressing as your skills develop. If you proceed this way and make a mistake, you are much less likely to do yourself terminal financial damage.

ㅂ ㅂ ㅂ

Now we're going to meet Troy H. He's going to tell us about one of his recent development deals, and also share how he works out his figures and is developing his property investing system.

Real deal: developing my system

Hi, my name is Troy. I've been married for about five years to my lovely wife and we have two darling daughters; the youngest one has just started crawling, so nothing in the house is safe any more.

I'm a self-employed property investor. I came to property almost by accident. I was running a retail store which wasn't going too well. A decision had to be made as to whether to keep the store or try something else, or — heaven forbid — go and get a job. We eventually sold the shop, and about this time we also happened to settle on our first investment property.

My strategy

In one of my very early deals, I spent three months buried among tools, timber and nails, and managing the tradies. I felt like I lost touch with the market during this time because I was focusing on doing the work. I knew I couldn't keep doing this. I needed to spend more time finding and managing the deals rather than doing the physical work, so I chose development as a strategy.

I was very nervous at the beginning so I started in regional Victoria. I was very worried about all the things that I thought could go wrong so I wanted to start small. It was cheaper to buy and to build there, so I thought that if I completely stuffed it up the damage would be limited. My first development property cost $133 000, and I put a small unit on the back. I figured that at that price you can't really lose too much money.

However, early on in that deal I began to think that maybe I did actually know what I was doing, so I bought another one. This really started the investment process for me. I now call that first deal my apprenticeship — like an apprentice I didn't make much money but I learnt a lot.

My deal

In this deal we undertook a development in the eastern suburbs of Melbourne. We bought an old house and knocked it over, and we built three townhouses on the land which was nearly 900 square metres.

It was covered in trees and I think that scared a lot of other developers away, but we did our due diligence and found that the trees weren't of much concern and we could get three homes on there. We crunched our numbers and came to the conclusion that it would be a profitable deal. We negotiated a 120-day settlement.

On the road to financial freedom ...

A long settlement is a great idea when you have to make submissions to the council. The vendor still holds the property, but you can get started on the work without any holding costs.

When the project was complete we sold all of the homes to first home buyers, for a little over $1.5 million. This was very exciting, and the profit figure is only a few thousand away from what we expected from our due diligence. It gave us a lot of confidence in our ability to make this work again and again.

I've actually been quite good at determining the expected profit in my deals because I put a lot of time and effort into working this out. The selling price is the one key component of your figures that you don't have control over, so I put in the time and effort to come up with an accurate figure. I work out what I expect a property will sell for and then work backwards from there to calculate the figures.

I work out three sets of numbers for every deal. The first is what I expect the end product would sell for at the current time. That's my most important figure, and I use it to crunch my numbers.

The second figure I calculate is what the property might sell for when I actually come to sell it, which might be in 12 or 18 months. This is a higher figure; however, it isn't an important figure in my calculations. I think too many developers focus on a higher future sale price, but if they encounter a flat market they run into trouble, and make a loss.

I also work out a worst-case scenario bottom line, which is what would happen if the global financial crisis came back on steroids and everything collapsed in a flaming heap. I calculate whether I could still sell and at least break even if this happened.

On the road to financial freedom...

If your end profit is very close to your expected profit, you have analysed that deal well. If the expected profit is a long way from expectations, look at your numbers again to see where you went wrong and make every effort to learn about what you need to do differently. Remember, it's all about the numbers.

The figures

The figures for this deal are shown in table 14.1.

Table 14.1: real deal figures

Purchase price	$445 000
Closing costs	$22 000
Length of project	18 months
Plans and permits	$22 000
Construction costs	$584 000
Interest costs	$45 000
Selling costs	$6 000
Other costs	$153 000
Sale price	$1 500 000
Total profit	**$223 000**

I took out a loan from the bank to fund the construction costs, but due to reduced lending currently available from the banks I was still a little bit short so I took on a couple of private investors to make up the difference. The interest cost in the figures includes interest paid to those investors.

The selling costs are low because we ended up selling the homes ourselves. This keeps costs down, but the price is high. For example, there are early starts on freezing Saturday mornings to open the property for inspection and you also have to handle the constant enquiries from potential buyers and ongoing questions from the eventual purchasers. This is where the agents earn their money! We saved a bit of money but it took up a lot of time which could have been used looking for our next project, so I would prefer not to use this approach in the future.

My investing system

I like to have a number of deals on the go at once, and I stagger them so that they are not all at the same stage. This allows me to run multiple deals simultaneously, and as one deal is finishing another is starting. I can keep control over the work so that things don't get out of hand, and this approach also allows me to keep control of the finances.

We don't have any fancy tricks for finding deals — our main method is to work the agents very hard. My partner is great at this, and visits all the good agents in an area where we are looking and keeps at them. He meets them and calls them regularly, even if they don't call back (which is a common occurrence) — he makes sure they don't forget about us, and gives them a clear outline of what we are looking for so that they can do the work for us.

When we first started the global financial situation was a little bit more comfortable, so I didn't have a lot of problem financing my first few deals. But then I bought my fourth deal on a 30-day settlement, to lock away a good deal before anyone else could see it, assuming that I wouldn't have any problem with finance — but the bank said no!

Uh oh!

I had a property settling in a couple of weeks and I wasn't sure where the money was coming from. This caused a few sleepless nights but fortunately we found a good mortgage broker who saved the day.

That was a real wake-up call for us, though; we realised that we couldn't keep going using just our own money, so we started to look for private investors who wanted to invest a set amount of money for a set interest rate return that was better than the banks were offering for term deposits. This allowed us to do more projects than we would be able to otherwise, and it gives our investors a good return. It's very difficult to do multiple development deals without an alternative source of funds, and this has worked well for us.

I always hire a builder for my deals. I am often asked why I don't become a registered builder and do the work myself. I don't have the time to do this; I pay a builder to do the work, and look after and coordinate the tradies. I spend my time managing my deals on a macro level, not on a micro level. I believe that the profit is made in finding the right sites and putting the highest and best use development on the site, so that's where I spend most of my time.

Some developers don't sell until completion, with the argument being they will get a better price when there is something to see for the buyer to fall in love with. While that may potentially be true, we believe in the 'bird in the hand' theory and commence selling as soon as the planning permit is approved. We have found we do not need to discount the price to get pre-sales, and they make bank finance much easier too. Finally, having a project completely sold off the plan makes me a lot more comfortable buying the next projects before completion of current ones.

When we are selling completed properties I always stage them. I've bought a heap of cheap furniture that I just pull out when I need to stage a property. It would not last long in normal use, but when you are staging that's all you need. I think this is a vital part of the selling process. We also hire a colour consultant to help us select the best colours for the properties, and find that the purchasers love the results.

On the road to financial freedom...

When selling multiple properties, it can be a good idea to have a similar colour scheme in all of them. This allows you to use the same furniture to stage each one.

I feel like I've created a good backbone for my investing. It gives me a good structure to work around, but it's flexible when I need it to be as well.

I'm also constantly seeking better ways to do things. I certainly don't know everything, so I spend a lot of time sharing ideas and talking to other people who know more than I do so that I can build my knowledge. I go to open inspections and chase people around and ask them what they like and don't like about the house. These are the buyers I am trying to appeal to—it's a great way to get valuable insights. And I'm always looking to be able to build the same product more cheaply, or to get a better result while spending the same amount on building costs.

My tips for other investors

My tips for other investors are:

➤ Be very thorough in your due diligence; if you aren't thorough you are gambling.

➤ You don't know it all, and can't do it all. Be willing to pay experts for their knowledge and experience.

➤ Have a mentor; they are the most valuable member of your team.

➤ Always start with the end result in mind and figure out what needs to be done to get there.

➤ Don't be intimidated by developing. If you can complete a reno, you can complete a development. It's a similar process.

➤ Set goals. If you don't know where you are going, how are you going to get there?

My current situation

For me financial freedom doesn't mean mansions or Ferraris. I like to have free time to spend with my growing family, and this is what real estate investing gives me. I'm happy to keep working on my investing because I enjoy it, and you have to do something with your time so I may as well keep doing this.

Looking to the future

I'm currently looking for three- to five-unit sites. Down the track I might look at some larger developments, but basically we are happy with how things are going and will continue with this system for the foreseeable future.

We would like to be able to do an additional two or three projects per year, and to do this we will need to finetune our system a bit more. I want to spend a bit less time on the actual development and more time finding deals. I can do this if I automate things a little bit more.

🏠 🏠 🏠

Troy is focusing on his *system*, not each individual deal. He has built his system over a number of years and deals, as he discovers what works and what doesn't, and he is always looking to refine it further.

Do something!

You need to be an expert in your strategy to develop a successful system. To take stock of your level of knowledge of your strategy, describe in detail the following:

- how the strategy works
- the outcome of the strategy

- the numbers of the strategy

- the time frames

- the people required to make the strategy work

- the language involved with the strategy

- the areas where the strategy will produce the greatest profit.

If there are any areas that you don't know enough about, research them to improve your knowledge.

Bonus content

To hear Troy speak about his deal in more detail, go to <www.resultsmentoring.com/book1/>.

Chapter 15

Passive income and financial freedom

Let's fast-forward a few years...

You've determined your goals and strategies, and bought and sold your way through multiple properties. By now your system is probably working well and you are making some good money from your investing. Now you have to make a choice. If you are enjoying what you are doing and want to keep going, then great! That's what you should do.

But at some point you may want to pack it all up and take a break—this usually means retiring! To be able to do this you will need a stream of income that requires minimal time input from you.

Hands off, cash flow

Cash/equity requirements
- High amount of money required but that's okay ... you have lots of it available

Borrowing capacity requirements
- Low: income from your investments more than covers any debt-servicing requirements

Complexity/risk
- Low/medium complexity, low/medium risk as you now employ people to manage your property and projects

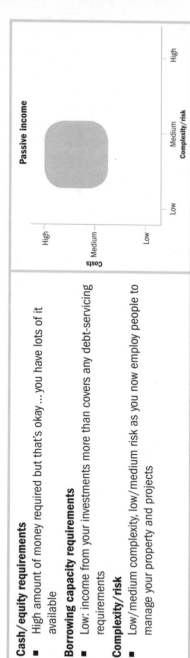

Skills requirements
- High ability to relax
- A high level of people management skills are required, but that's okay because by now you are an expert
- Detailed knowledge of chosen strategies remains essential

Time requirements
- Low time needed to manage system due to delegation of day-to-day management tasks

Desired outcome
- Ongoing passive income that exceeds living expenses – financial freedom!

Make no mistake—no investment or source of income is completely time free (except perhaps a term deposit, but there is a problem with relying on term deposits, as you will see later). All investments require input at some point: do I sell it? Do I change it? Do I reinvest? You can never walk away completely. But your primary focus at this point may be to minimise the amount of time you have to spend on your investing.

What is passive income?

Passive income means generating a net positive (surplus) income from the assets you have accumulated, without any significant involvement or work by you. In property investing, your assets would be the wealth you have created over the years doing deals such as renovations, developments and subdivisions, or the equity you've built up in properties you have held. After investing successfully for a number of years you will probably be in a position where you have built up a large capital base and can use this to generate a passive income, so that you no longer have to work in a job or even keep actively turning over deals, but it doesn't mean that you'll never have to 'lift a finger' again.

Why?

For example, if you have $2 million available and you put it in a 10-year term deposit earning 5 per cent, you will earn $100 000 a year for virtually no effort—you just have to open the account. If you need $100 000 per year to support your lifestyle then this income will give you financial freedom! You will be able to live your life without having to work. Right?

Well, unfortunately it's not quite as simple as this. Your $100 000 won't buy you as much in 10 years' time as it does now because of inflation. If prices double roughly every 10 years, a loaf of bread that costs you $2 now will cost you $4 in 10 years' time. Eventually this $100 000 won't be enough to live on because the prices of everything will go up but you will still be earning $100 000 per annum. And if you simply leave your money in the term deposit and withdraw the interest, the amount of money in the account is not going to grow either.

On the road to financial freedom...

If the value of an asset you own is not growing, you are actually going backwards because inflation means that as time goes by your money buys less.

One of the reasons that property is a choice of the rich for creating passive income is because it generally keeps up with or exceeds the rate of inflation.

Let's say that instead of putting your money into a 5 per cent term deposit, you bought four $500 000 properties outright with your $2 million. And let's assume that each property earned you about $500 in net rental income per week. Over a year this is about $100 000 — roughly the same as the term deposit.

The key difference is that property values go up over time, whereas the money in the term deposit does not. So in 10 years your asset base could go from $2 million in four $500 000 houses to $4 million in four $1 million houses, without you doing much at all. The rent is also likely to increase; in fact it may also have doubled. So now instead of earning $100 000 per year you are earning $200 000 per year. With little effort you have doubled your asset base and your income in 10 years! And how much will that 5 per cent term deposit be earning in 10 years? Still $100 000.

In 10 years' time, when that loaf of bread costs $4 instead of $2, you will still be able to put the same amount of food on the table because your income has increased at the same rate as prices of goods, and you will still be financially free.

Now that we've established that property can help you not just achieve financial freedom but also maintain it, what *type* of property should you be looking at for your retirement?

No property purchase is completely devoid of some ongoing effort or maintenance. So if you want to retire and do as little as possible then you need to look for properties that require low time commitments and limited management.

If you are dealing with Joe Average as a tenant in your residential property, things will go wrong with the property from time to time. The heater breaks, the roof leaks, the gate falls off the hinges or the air-conditioner stops working. All of these things are going to require your attention, because in Australia and New Zealand it is the landlord's responsibility to maintain a residential rental property. This requires time, effort and cost.

Fortunately there is a type of property investment that is less demanding and can even give a better income return.

Using commercial property for passive income

Commercial property is everywhere and anywhere you find businesses. This includes shops, office blocks, warehouses and factories. Most businesses don't own their premises but instead rent them from commercial property investors. Investing in commercial property is often the end point of the property investing journey, which may have started with a simple rental house or a cosmetic reno.

Commercial versus residential

Table 15.1 (overleaf) shows some of the key reasons that commercial property is usually more desirable than residential property if you are seeking low-stress passive income.

More importantly, perhaps, residential rental returns near a CBD vary depending upon economic climates, but generally hover between 3 per cent and 6 per cent. Commercial properties in the same area may get a rental return of 6 per cent to 8 per cent or even higher, so you will earn more for every dollar invested. This means that to earn your $100 000 income you don't need $2 million, you might need only $1.5 million or $1.8 million. Or, if you do have $2 million, your income will be around $120 000 or $140 000 per year.

Table 15.1: commercial property versus residential property

Commercial property	Residential property
Tenants usually pay the outgoings (rates, insurance and so on)	Landlord pays the outgoings (rates, insurance and so on)
Rent is usually indexed for inflation and automatically reviewed to market	Landlord must initiate rental review and increases are generally less tolerated
Less emotional – investors operate within industry rules	More emotional as clients (tenants) rent their homes
Value and capital growth determined based on rents and the quality of the tenant	Value harder to determine and more influenced by emotional factors (e.g. desirability of location)
Governed by lease and common (contract) law	Governed by lease and residential tenancies law
Multi-year leases are common and often include options to extend lease	Leases are normally for a fixed term of 12 months or less
Tenants are businesses, usually with a vested interest in looking after the property	Tenants are individuals, who might trash your property
Leasehold improvements made by tenant (e.g. fit out)	Improvements made by landlord (e.g. new carpet)
Less need for a property manager	Time-intensive property management requirements

The advantages of commercial property investing

Some of the major advantages of commercial property if you are seeking passive income include the following:

➤ Longer leases. Businesses prefer not to move. They like to be in the same location because their customers know where they are. Commercial leases usually span multiple years and may include options to renew the lease at the end of each term, for example 3+3+3 (meaning a three-year lease with two more three-year options) or 5+5+5. If you can get a major corporation as a client, you might even get a 30-year lease (10+10+10)!

➤ Fewer vacancies because of longer leases.

➤ You can negotiate lease agreements with tenants so that they are responsible for all outgoings, including rates, insurances, repairs and maintenance. In a residential rental, if the kitchen needs replacing this is your job. In a commercial property such things are typically the responsibility of the tenant. Less overheads mean that you get to keep more of the rent.

➤ Business tenants tend to look after their premises better, especially if it's a shop front or an office. When was the last time you heard of a commercial tenant trashing their place?

➤ Commercial tenants often pay for the fit out of their own premises, meaning there is little need for the landlord to spend on renovating the inside of the property.

On the road to financial freedom...

The rent on a commercial property is usually based on floor space (square metres), not the number of rooms or style of property as it is with residential property.

The disadvantages of commercial property investing

With all of these advantages, there must be some downsides—and there are:

➤ Businesses suffer in economic downturns, and can go bust. Small businesses usually run into problems first, which means your leases could be abruptly broken if the business folds.

➤ If your tenant's business fails then no matter what the lease says you are unlikely to get much rent out of them.

➤ Vacancies can be longer. They are fewer, but when they occur they can be longer because the market of commercial tenants is much smaller than the residential market. Commercial vacancies can be as little as three months at a time or as much as years in poor economic circumstances or if your property serves a specific purpose.

On the road to financial freedom...

Residential tenancy laws do not apply to commercial property. Any disputes are settled in court.

So you can see there are some added risks that you don't have to worry about with residential property. But this is why the returns tend to be higher.

What are the commercial property options?

So what is the ideal commercial property?

Rural industrial estates? The yields will be higher but there is a greater risk of vacancy because the demand from businesses for such locations is low.

CBD industrial estates? CBD locations are more expensive to get into, but there will usually be fewer, shorter vacancies. The higher purchase price will give you a slightly lower yield, but the vacancy risk is reduced. This might be the better option if you want to worry less about holding an empty property.

What if you buy a single floor in an office building and then lease it out? A downside of office blocks is that new blocks are always being built, so tenants always have the option of moving to a better, more modern building. And offices—in comparison to retail outlets—are usually less dependent on location, so the business might be more likely to move.

On the road to financial freedom...

A commercial property is just a 'shell'. It's up to the tenant to fit the property out to meet their requirements, at their expense.

Another option is a retail outlet. The best location to buy such a property is usually in a highly populated growth corridor shopping strip where there is no more room for commercial outlets; for example, Swan St in Richmond in Melbourne or the Bondi shopping strip in Sydney. Such strips are very popular with consumers so there will always be demand from retailers for stores in these strips. This demand means there will be low vacancies, but also that such properties will cost you more to buy. With $2 million you might be able to buy only one property, whereas you might be able to buy four properties in other, lower demand locations.

As you might guess from all this, a higher rental return usually comes with a higher risk of vacancy—such as in a rural estate—while a lower return usually comes with a lower risk of vacancy—such as in a high-demand shopping strip. It's up to you to decide what mix is right for you.

The more properties you have, the less risk there is to your income. If you buy one $2 million property and your tenant moves out, your income ceases until you find a new tenant. If you have four properties and one tenant moves out, you will still have three-quarters of your income until a new tenant moves in.

On the road to financial freedom...

The strength of a commercial lease depends on the strength of the tenant. Strong businesses make good tenants. Poorly run businesses are more likely to go under and you will be left looking for a new tenant, so understanding a tenant's business should be a central part of your due diligence before taking on the tenant.

A lot more to know

Commercial property investing is a vast topic worthy of a book all on its own. We've included a brief discussion here simply to give you an idea of how you can create an ongoing passive income stream for your financial future.

You don't *have* to retire...

Many people who have attained this level with their investing reach a point where they have the option to retire. Troy H from the previous chapter will have to face this choice in the not-too-distant future. His system is evolving. But he is beginning to question whether he actually wants to pack it in. You will notice a few of the investors in the book have said that even when they reach the point of not having to work, they will keep investing because they enjoy it and it gives them a sense of purpose in life. For some people, sitting on the beach all day in luxury would actually get boring.

The choice is yours. You will have noticed throughout the book that it's vital to make choices that suit you and your circumstances, and this one is no different.

On the road to financial freedom...

Passive income is a great goal and it is achievable, but that doesn't mean you have to retire. Think about what you will do when you reach the point that you no longer have to work for a living.

Do something!

Do some research on commercial properties. Find examples of different types (for example, industrial, office and retail), and look at the different rental returns. Compare the figures. What sort of commercial property appeals most to you? Why?

Chapter 16

Your next step ...

Welcome to the end of the book! Congratulations on making it this far—we hope you have learnt a lot in these pages, and gained some motivation from the stories that each of the investors in this book have shared.

You're reading this book for a reason. Perhaps you've started to feel that you aren't getting as much as you could out of life. Maybe you feel like you don't have enough money or time, or both.

Well, you're not alone. This is how many people come to real estate investing, because property has a great potential to give you back your life and allow you to reach your goals.

Many active investors begin their journey with smaller cash lump-sum deals such as cosmetic renovations or small subdivisions. There is no reason you can't do the same. This allows you to steadily build your capital with each deal. As your skills and available funds grow, you might want to move on to larger deals that generate larger profits. The eventual goal is to have enough capital built up so that you can buy enough assets to generate a passive income for the rest of your life.

At this point you've made it!

What happens then is up to you. You can sit on the beach all day, you can travel around the world on a skateboard, or you can keep investing just because you enjoy it—the options are almost endless because you know that the money will keep coming in but you only have to check on your investments occasionally.

And yes, it is possible. People just like you are in this book, sharing their experiences and getting closer every day to the life they dream of.

> **On the road to financial freedom...**
>
> ...you can find the life you have always wanted.

Did you notice?

Throughout this book we've not only offered you examples of how people have undertaken various property investing strategies, but we've also offered you a series of tasks and questions designed to get you moving along a path of property investing that best suits you. This was deliberate, as was the order of those questions.

Here is a brief summary of the process we have outlined in this book, in the sequence that they appeared in the book:

1   What is your end game, your *why*? Take some time out and try to figure out what it is that you want to get from putting all this effort into your investing.

2   From your end game, work backwards and see if you can determine the shorter term goals that will help you reach your end goal. Drill down until you figure out what you might need to do in the next 12 months, then six months, and so on.

3   It's now time to look at your financial situation to determine what you have to play with. How much cash do you have at your fingertips? How much equity can you get your hands on? And how much will you be able to borrow? Support your financial awareness by creating a budget, and make changes to your lifestyle if you need to free up more cash to get started.

4   Do a skills assessment. It's now time to see what skills you have that will support a successful property deal. What are you good at? (Strengths.) What do you enjoy? (Passion.) And what do you prefer not to do? (Weaknesses to delegate!)

5   Relative to your 12-month goal, take a second to declare what it is that you seek from your next property investing deal: cash flow or a lump-sum cash gain.

6   Also determine whether you want to be hands on or hands off.

7   Study the property market. While it might seem to have little to do with completing the deal, your understanding of the property market in your area is a critical part of the success of your deal. What's happening in the market, locally and overseas? Where are we in the economic cycle?

8   Based upon your knowledge of the market, your desired financial outcome, your strengths and weaknesses, and your budget, available cash and borrowing capacity, choose a strategy that is right for you.

9   Get to know the numbers of your strategy relative to your circumstances! We can not stress this enough. Given we are talking about creating wealth, knowing the numbers of a deal intimately is critical!

10 With your accumulated knowledge to this point, it's time for you to create a description of your ideal property.

11 Now it's time to get out there and start looking! Consider the suburbs that are more likely to work for your chosen strategy and your numbers, then thoroughly get to know those areas.

12 You're about ready to buy now; it's time to build your team.

13 Hit the streets to find and buy your property!

14 If you've done all the work above, your plan for this deal should be clear ... it's now just a matter of following through on the plan.

15 Repeat!!

16 Get better at it and very soon a system will begin to evolve. Create and refine your system.

17 Retire — or not! But it's nice to have the choice!

Your next step is...

... to get out there and get started!

There is only one person who can make this happen for you. You see this person in the bathroom mirror each morning. We can help you with the knowledge and you can learn from the experiences of others, but we can't make it happen for you. If you follow this process, put in the effort and keep going you will get where you want to go. This is what the investors in this book are doing, and will continue to do until they arrive at their final destination! Remember, they all began from different points, and they are all at different stages along the road, but they are all pursuing their dreams.

To help you take those first steps, here's a 21-day plan designed to get you going:

Let's start by identifying some goals:

➤ *21-day goal*: to have found an area that I can begin to look in for the deal that I know will make the profit/cash flow I want.

➤ *Seven-day goal:* to have done steps 1 to 6 above. *'Get "clear" on me!'*

Now let's create the daily tasks:

➤ *Day 1:*

△ *Task 1.* Put aside two uninterrupted hours today to sit down and reflect about your life.

△ *Task 2.* At the start of your two-hour window, go to a park with some paper and write down what is important in your life, and how you want it to be better. Put a 'line in the sand' representing the specific date (day, month and year) when you want to be living this life (realistically), and write it down.

△ *Task 3.* In the last 20 minutes of this two-hour block, look at the weeks ahead and plan to put aside 20 minutes a day for yourself, for the next 21 days.

△ *Task 4.* Consider finding a mentor. Who do you know who has done the kinds of things you want to do with your own investing?

➤ *Day 2.* When your 20-minute break starts, take your piece of paper from yesterday and take a second look at it. Spend the whole 20 minutes going through what you have written and see if it still rings true for you.

If so, commit to making the changes and sacrifices that are needed to make your desired future happen!

➤ If not, then repeat yesterday's exercise! Once you are comfortable with your reasons for wanting to invest and the life you want to be leading (and by when), write it all down, and pin this up somewhere where you can see it daily.

➤ *Day 3.* When your 20-minute break starts, grab that same piece of paper and begin to work backwards from your 'line in the sand' to one year from now. What do you need to have achieved in 12 months to know you are working towards achieving your end game goal? And then ask, 'What do I need to have done in six months to feel confident that I'll achieve my 12 month goal?' Keep working backwards from six months, to three months, to one month and then seven days from now, defining what you think you'll need to have achieved at each milestone.

On the road to financial freedom...

In your planning, remember to allow at least three to six months for getting ready to buy. It's surprising the amount of time it takes to get ready to buy with confidence. Persistence is the key.

➤ *Day 4.* When your 20-minute break starts, grab a different piece of paper and begin to look at your finances. Grab your bank statements and write down your account balances, credit card debts and limits. Write down all outstanding loan amounts, including house, car and personal loans. Also write down your various assets (do not include furniture, cars or anything you're not willing to sell for your property investing; the house is okay to list because banks let you borrow against some of the equity in it). Add up your cash, assets and liabilities.

Make an appointment to go and speak to a mortgage broker next week.

➤ *Day 5*. When your 20-minute break starts, grab another piece of paper and begin to reflect on what you enjoy doing. Write down a description of the sorts of things you enjoy doing at home, at work, and throughout life. Also write down the things you don't enjoy doing.

➤ *Day 6*. When your 20-minute break starts, grab yesterday's piece of paper and keep working on that. Re-read your notes from yesterday, and add anything else that comes to mind. The idea is to come to some conclusion about what you are willing to do, and not do, with your investing. Now it's time to combine some of your thoughts from what you have written over the last few days. Do you want to do a project for cash flow or a lump-sum amount of cash? Do you want to be hands on or hands off with this deal? Create a shortlist of strategies that you might like to attempt — say, about three.

➤ *Day 7*. When your 20-minute break starts answer the following questions: Did you achieve your seven-day goal? Did you get through steps 1 to 6? Now, plan for 20 minutes per day for the next seven days ... Set your next seven-day goal: to spend 20 minutes a day for the next seven days learning more about the property market. This is aimed at helping you through steps 7 and 8 above. Log into <www.sophisticatedpropertyinvestor.com> and read the latest newsletter about what's happening in the property market and to get more information on property investing. Plan to buy some major newspapers each day next week.

➤ *Day 8*. Remember to buy a newspaper today. See if your newsagent also has the local community paper and pick up a copy of that too. When your 20-minute break starts, open the newspaper and begin to look for commentary about the economy in your area. Read three articles about the economy or property market. Log into <www.sophisticatedpropertyinvestor.com> and read one of the back issues of the newsletter. Remember also to meet with your mortgage broker this week. You need to know how much you can borrow.

➤ *Day 9*. Remember to buy a newspaper today. When your 20-minute break starts, open the newspaper and begin to look for commentary about the economy in your area. Find and read at least three articles about the economy or property market. Log into <www.sophisticatedpropertyinvestor.com> and read one of the back issues of the newsletter.

➤ *Day 10*. Remember to buy a newspaper today. When your 20-minute break starts, open the newspaper and begin to look for commentary about the economy in your area. Find and read at least three articles about the economy or property market. Log into <www.sophisticatedpropertyinvestor.com> and read one of the back issues of the newsletter. Do you feel you are getting a better picture about what's happening in your area, and the property market as a whole?

➤ *Day 11*. Remember to buy a newspaper today. When your 20-minute break starts, open the newspaper and begin to look for commentary about the economy in your area. Find and read at least three articles about the economy or property market. Log into <www.sophisticatedpropertyinvestor.com> and read another one of the back issues of the newsletter. If you do not feel you are growing wiser about the market, buy a different paper or do some additional research (like checking out your bank's website for their own economic commentary).

➤ *Day 12.* Remember to buy a newspaper today. If you haven't yet picked up a copy of your local community paper, then be sure to do that too. When your 20-minute break starts, open the newspaper and begin to look for commentary about the economy in your area. Find and read at least three articles about the economy or property market. Log into <www.sophisticatedpropertyinvestor. com> and read another one of the back issues of the newsletter. Write down what you think is occurring in the economy and property market in your local area, in the broader region, and across the country—are property values going up, down or sideways?

➤ *Day 13.* Remember to buy a newspaper today. When your 20-minute break starts, open the newspaper and begin to look for commentary about the economy in your area. Find and read at least three articles about the economy or property market. Do they confirm your thoughts from yesterday? Now is the time to finalise your strategy decision. Based upon your conclusions from last week, and the economic research from this week, choose a strategy from your shortlist that you think best suits you! Write it down, and pin it up somewhere where you can see it daily.

➤ *Day 14.* When your 20-minute break starts, answer the following questions: Did you achieve your seven-day goal? Did you get through steps 7 and 8 above? Now, plan for 20 minutes per day for the next seven days... Set your next seven-day goal: to spend 20 minutes a day for the next seven days learning more about the numbers for my chosen strategy. This is aimed at helping you through steps 9 and 10 above. Having made the decision about the strategy that best suits you, revisit the chapter in this book about that strategy. Check your skills against the description at the start of the chapter. If the marriage is about right, well done! Re-read the chapter and download the recorded interview. Study this real deal well!

➤ *Day 15*. When your 20-minute break starts, copy the numbers and descriptions of those numbers for the 'real deal' of your chosen strategy onto a piece of paper. This can form a simple template for you to assess the figures for your circumstances. Set it up as it was done in chapter 6. Using this as a guide, set up the numbers for your circumstances. Start listing out any categories of cost or other figures that you're uncertain of. Take your time with this.

➤ *Day 16*. When your 20-minute break starts, go back to your numbers. Your job now is to come up with the model that suits your circumstances relative to the cash you have available and your borrowing capacity. Are you making any assumptions about the value you are relying on? Can you come up with any ideas on how you might go about researching the costs and other figures relevant to your strategy? Can you think of who might have some of the answers? If so, call them to find out the truth. Every assumption you make here increases the risk of loss. Again, take your time with this. It's important to get it right. (This is where a mentor comes in really handy!)

➤ *Day 17*. When your 20-minute break starts, go back to your numbers. Now you have applied your circumstances to your strategy. Here are the critical questions: How much do you need to buy your property for? How much do you need to sell OR rent it for, in order to make the profit or cash flow that you seek? Again, take your time with this. It's important to get this right.

➤ *Day 18*. When your 20-minute break starts, go back to the work you did to determine your preferred strategy. Relative to this work, and your numbers, take some time to write down a description of your ideal property, highlighting the characteristics you would be looking for to suit your strategy and profit objectives.

➤ *Day 19.* When your 20-minute break starts, look again at your numbers. By now you would be pretty clear on them (even if it's taken longer than 19 days). It's now time to make up your version of the '15-minute suburb search'! Re-read chapter 7 and study how the 15-minute suburb search works for a Cosmetic Reno. Apply a similar approach for your chosen strategy using the key details of purchase price and selling price OR rental value. Do your 15-minute suburb search as described in chapter 7!

➤ *Day 20.* When your 20-minute break starts, jump on <www.realestate.com.au> or <www.realestate.co.nz> and begin to look in your preferred suburb for properties that meet the criteria you defined back on Day 18. Note down the asking prices and the contact details of the real estate agents listing those properties. Next, consider the type of property that you are thinking of selling OR renting back to the market. Look for examples of these properties for sale or rent in your selected area on <www.realestate. com.au> or <www.realestate.co.nz>, and note down the asking prices or asking rents as applicable to your strategy. Compare these figures to the purchase prices of the properties you found that met your criteria. Taking into account what you know about the costs involved for your chosen strategy, does it seem likely that this suburb will satisfy your profit/cash flow outcomes? If yes, get ready, you are about to hit the streets and meet some real estate agents. If not, begin reviewing the next suburb on your list.

➤ *Day 21.* When your 20-minute break starts, call the list of agents you noted yesterday! Make appointments to go and see the houses that fit your criteria. When the time is right ... get in the car and go!

(Note: this a guide only, and the days are less relevant than your constant application to the process. If this series of tasks takes you 40, 60 or 100 days to complete, it doesn't matter. The completion of the tasks is what is important.)

🏠 🏠 🏠

As a parting thought, we want you to know that real estate investing can provide you with opportunities you might only dream of now. Believe in yourself, and you will achieve the life you so desire.

We hope you have found this book inspirational, useful and enjoyable, and that you have gained some valuable knowledge and insights. We wish you all the best with your investing. And we look forward to meeting up with you along the road to financial freedom!

Index